PINT TO
PINT

About the authors

The 'Pint to Pint' column is written by a diverse selection of regular *Telegraph* journalists, among them beer experts, architecture buffs, walkers, rock critics, war correspondents, and scholars of this and that. The column enjoys many tens of thousands of fans and regularly receives letters from readers about its selections. A new pub is featured every Saturday.

The Telegraph

PINT TO PINT

A Crawl Around Britain's Best Pubs

Published in the UK in 2016
by Icon Books Ltd, Omnibus Business Centre,
39–41 North Road, London N7 9DP
email: info@iconbooks.com
www.iconbooks.com

Sold in the UK, Europe and Asia
by Faber & Faber Ltd, Bloomsbury House,
74–77 Great Russell Street,
London WC1B 3DA or their agents

Distributed in the UK, Europe and Asia
by TBS Ltd, TBS Distribution Centre, Colchester Road,
Frating Green, Colchester CO7 7DW

Distributed in Australia and New Zealand
by Allen & Unwin Pty Ltd,
PO Box 8500, 83 Alexander Street,
Crows Nest, NSW 2065

Distributed in South Africa by
Jonathan Ball, Office B4, The District,
41 Sir Lowry Road, Woodstock 7925

Distributed in India by Penguin Books India,
7th Floor, Infinity Tower – C, DLF Cyber City,
Gurgaon 122002, Haryana

Distributed in Canada
by Publishers Group Canada,
76 Stafford Street, Unit 300
Toronto, Ontario M6J 2S1

ISBN: 978-178578-039-4
(Book People edition ISBN: 978-178578-089-9)

Typeset by Simmons Pugh
Printed and bound in the UK by Clays Ltd, St Ives plc

Contents

GREATER LONDON

EAST OF ENGLAND

WEST MIDLANDS 253

WALES 277

Publisher's Foreword

Welcome to *Pint to Pint*, a celebration of Britain's best-loved institution, the pub.

What makes a classic pub? There are as many answers to that as there are pub-goers, but some common ground can be found in all of them: they have a warm welcome, they get the beer right, they may well have good food (though it's not usually the sole focus of the pub), and they are places for convivial conversation or for peaceful contemplation, as you wish. Above all they have character – they are not an exercise in corporate blandness or desperate commercialism.

Seasoned pub fans know a good pub the moment they see one, but it always helps to have some insider knowledge. Here we rely on the *Telegraph*'s experts to do the hard work for us, testing each pub against the rigorous standards they have devised over years of pub visits.

We have arranged the pubs into a 'crawl' – not to be attempted in one go – starting in the far south-west of England and heading east towards London, then up through eastern England to Scotland before returning down the north-western side of England and into Wales. The crawl begins on Lundy Island in the Bristol Channel and ends at Porthcawl in South Wales, so if you want to complete the last 50 miles you will need to be a strong swimmer.

We hope you enjoy the trip, even if only from the comfort of your armchair, and will raise a glass with us to the continued existence of great pubs in hard times.

Pint to Pint: The Pub Crawl

South-West England

The Marisco Tavern
Lundy Island

Unsullied by the accoutrements of modern life, the Marisco Tavern is the sort of pub I fantasise about. Quiet, with a traditional but unique interior; no fruit machines, no music and no mobiles, tablets, laptops or gadgets of any kind, thanks to a ban that even someone as attached to their smartphone as I am will revel in.

Drinkers have spent some two hours crossing the Bristol Channel to get to Lundy, and another good half-hour climbing the steep road to the pub. By then they will have dropped back a gear or two to join the pace of island life. They do not want, nor need, to be bothered by the demands of email, texts, social media or other trivialities that detract from life's simpler pleasures – a pint of beer, chatting with your spouse, sharing time with friends or gazing at stunning views out to sea.

Remarkably for a remote island pub, there are three cask ales from which to choose. I order two pints of St Austell Black Prince (4%), a delicious creamy, chocolatey dark mild that is a rarity on the mainland. It is cool and perfectly kept. The Old Light ale (4.2%) is in similarly tip-top condition. Much later in the day, I'm tempted by a rum menu which boasts such gems as Pusser's Aged 15 Years and Mount Gay, of which the bartender unflinchingly inquires, 'Do you want it straight?'

The nautical decor includes an alarming collection of lifebelts bearing the name of ships wrecked on Lundy's shores, and the date they met their fate. The floor is made of slabs of granite from the island's quarries. Like all the best pubs there is a variety of seating: a long table for large groups or convivial eating, traditional tables and chairs and cosy benched booths with sea views. It even has a mezzanine. Not that it is so pretentious as to call it that.

Whether you've walked directly from the landing place or been for a yomp around the island you're bound to have worked up an appetite. The Tavern's menu ranges from cheesy chips (the perfect lunch when arriving during winter – the helicopter drops you off almost at the pub door) via baguettes and jacket potatoes through to seasonally changing dishes prepared from an impressive range of meat reared on the island (prices vary but mains start at £8.20). Lundy lamb is among the leanest you'll come across; Soay sheep are also resident, their meat is darker, gamier and full-flavoured thanks to a diet of turf and aromatic plants; venison is from the Sika deer population and Lundy pork sausages are available thanks to pigs imported as part of a sustainable waste-management programme.

The Marisco is a microcosm of Lundy's character. An island out of time, nobly resisting those elements of the 21st century it sees no point in; a genuine respite from the rat race.

Sophie Atherton, 17 August 2013

High Street, Lundy Island, Bristol Channel EX39 2LY (01237 431831); landmarktrust.org.uk/Lundyisland; opening times vary with the boat/helicopter timetable

The Minerva Inn
Plymouth

The sign at the door is a testament to the Minerva Inn's history: 'Home to the Press Gang' says the proud white lettering. For this tiny Plymouth pub was once the place where unfortunate souls had the king's shilling slipped into their pints, then found themselves huckled through a secret passage and 'impressed' on to a Royal Navy ship waiting on the nearby Barbican dockside.

Established somewhere around 1540, the Min claims to be the pilgrim city's oldest hostelry. It lies a short stroll from the Barbican, on a steeply graded cobbled street which was once home to Sir Francis Drake (he is said to have quaffed a gallon at the Minerva after defeating the Armada). An exquisite stained-glass depiction of a helmeted Minerva (the Roman goddess of wisdom) on the pub's one window is a relic from the time it was owned by the Octagon Brewery. The pub's hanging signage features an owl and refers to Hegel's idea that you only apprehend the historical moment you're living through as it comes to a close: 'The owl of Minerva spreads its wings only with the falling of the dusk.' Classy.

It can be a squeeze to get through the Min's skinny and low-ceilinged space to the bar; and you might need to breathe in just that little bit more if you're seeking refuge in the snug at the back bar – with its large open fire, sofas and artefacts relating to the pub's history. Originally the home of an Elizabethan sea captain, the Minerva was built using timber reclaimed from galleons belonging to the vanquished Armada. Part of one of the ship's spars forms the core of a spiral staircase.

Until recently, the ceiling was covered in the signatures of celebrities, servicemen and your ordinary punter, but local health and safety officials proclaimed the paint a fire hazard and ordered that it all be covered in something more flame retardant. But the tradition has started all over again.

On a Saturday afternoon there's a crowd of ex-Royal Navy guys who are a wee bit boisterous, but we can still chat quietly and try some of the ales: regulars Doom Bar and Tribute Cornish Pale Ale and guests including Camerons IPA, Dartmoor IPA and Hoppy Days from Devon's Bays – a does-what-it-says-on-the-tin short-time brew using green hops. Old Rosie, a honeyed, cloudy, unfiltered scrumpyish cider is a joy.

An enthusiastic local at the bar shows me a chink in the wall that is said to be part of the smuggling tunnel, and a peephole they say was used by the Press Gang to spot their prey coming. He sips a little more of his pint then whispers as he tells me of the time he nodded a hello to a man passing his back. 'I never believed in ghosts, but I saw the man pass. The bartender didn't,' he explains. 'Obviously it hasn't stopped me coming back.'

Audrey Gillan, 28 December 2013

31 Looe St, Plymouth PL4 0EA (01752 223047);
www.minervainn.co.uk

The Hyde Park Microbrewery
Plymouth

I n the midst of swirling traffic, in a not entirely auspicious part of the city, is one of Plymouth's oldest pubs. It doesn't have an award-winning heritage interior or a Michelin-starred chef but it does have something more important: charisma. Crossing the threshold, I feel a little like the Doctor stepping out of the Tardis.

It seems I've been transported to the pleasant, cosy dinginess of a traditional Eighties pub, before the marketing men rebranded them and brought in silly names. The walls and shelves are full of 'breweriana' celebrating the good, the bad and the ugly of the industry's history. You can even get a pint of Double Diamond or Watney's Red Barrel (but, now as then, why would you, especially since there is a microbrewery on site and a decent selection of other local cask ales at the bar?).

I order a pint of the pub's own Made in Mutley (4.8%), keenly priced at £2.50. It's a light floral bitter with a pleasant biscuity aftertaste. Other cask ales are £3.50 a pint and include the seemingly ubiquitous Sharp's Doom Bar, as well as several beers from Dartmoor Brewery, including its rather underrated, but very good, IPA.

The time-warp theme continues on screens, dotted around the bar, showing adverts from the Seventies and Eighties. A youthful, long-haired Terry Wogan advertises Currys; people are putting tigers in their tanks and a woman in a hazy field of poppies takes a break from her watercolour painting for a flaky bar of chocolate.

It all adds to the pleasing sense of nostalgia inside the

Hyde Park and makes me glad the pub was saved from being turned into an estate agent's office. It was listed as an Asset of Community Value after hundreds of locals signed a petition, and has been reinvigorated as a thriving boozer.

Thankfully, its retro theme doesn't extend to the food. Instead there's an extensive menu that owes more to American diners than it does to that Eighties staple chicken in a basket. There is everything from nachos and flatbreads, through burgers and pub classics such as bangers and mash, lasagne or pie and chips, with dozens of other options in between. Prices range from £3.95 for nachos to £12.95 for a mixed grill with sausages, gammon and steak from a local butchers. I opt for a tuna mayo sandwich and, too late, wish I had added a half pint of potatoes – a glorious stack of chips served in a beer mug (£1.50 for a half, £2.75 a pint).

The coming of craft beer seems to have brought with it a trend for hard seats that even the plumpest buttocks find miserable. The Hyde Park's seating offers a welcome return to tradition – plush and comfy, an ideal place to park your backside while you chat over a pint.

Sophie Atherton, 13 June 2015

88 Mutley Plain, Plymouth PL4 6JG (01752 601446); boutiquecoffeebrands.co.uk/thehydepark

The Cott Inn
Dartington, Devon

The Cott Inn slumps on a gentle slope, in a spruced-up hamlet just across the river from Dartington Hall, site of the Telegraph Ways With Words festival. It is elongated, cyclopean and slightly wonky, like a sleeping dinosaur. It has been open for trade since the 14th century, but the obligatory markers of antiquity – two inglenooks, copper pans, high-backed settles at every turn – are offset with little contemporary touches.

So those settles, which might easily induce a certain tenor of sobriety (they are more suited to adjudicating a witch trial than kicking back to enjoy a jazz set with a pint of real ale), are lightly strewn with Orla Kiely-esque cushions; and there are sparsely elegant flower arrangements in random bits of repurposed glassware on the tables.

Nevertheless, it is as the Platonic ideal of a venerable country pub that the Cott commends itself. It is made from impeccably traditional materials: the roof is thatch, and at least one wall is cob, a lumpy porridge of clay, straw, blood and other substances.

Two staircases up to a little row of bedrooms on the first floor are set into the thickness of the wall, and have doors at the bottom; using them confers a vaguely swashbuckling feeling, as if you were bursting free from the Château d'If rather than inquiring about the possibility of a full English for the following morning. There is the classic West British outside loo (which gives you a chance to admire a lovely little garden set in front of the pub).

The Cott's food looked wholesome and expertly prepared, but isn't particularly fancy or fashionable (sandwiches and fresh local fish at lunchtimes; hearty, traditional dishes and more fish in the evenings); the range of beers by no means as extensive as you'd find in many similar places. But I enjoyed my Denbury Dreamer, brewed either five or six miles away (the testimony of the bar staff varied); and I liked the look of an extensive wine list – though I didn't happen to notice whether the 'tonic wine' made at nearby Buckfast Abbey, such a success in the Scottish market, was on it.

As for atmosphere: well, the night I went, the atmosphere was what you might call 'jazzy', Sunday being live music night. For all I know, as a rule the bar is propped up with locals talking about the price of fish or the categorical imperative, or gazing ruminatively at their pints on the counter as if willing them to launch into a square-dance across its surface.

But I can report that it is a beautiful place, friendly and well-run – what's more, it's an easy half-hour's walk along a well-maintained riverside path from Totnes station, through woods and over water meadows, with the smell of the last wild garlic seeping from the damp greenery, and shards of quartz in the granite pebbles on the riverbed winking in the sunlight.

Keith Miller, 5 July 2014

Cott Lane, Dartington, Totnes, Devon TQ9 6HE (01803 863777); cottinn.co.uk

The Steam Packet Inn
Totnes, Devon

The New Age, upbeat spirit of Totnes is always apparent in summer. So we did wonder, flippantly, if the town's Steam Packet Inn might have a biodynamic wheat juice bar and ambient whale music. But no, just five minutes' walk from the long hair and rainbow pantaloons of the town centre we were in a different world of warehouse apartments, jolly boats, and a sunny and spacious pub terrace where the genteel (and older) crowd sip their sauv blanc in the sun.

Or, in our case, tackle a pint of refreshing, lemony Red Rock Pilsner made at the eponymous, tiny, four-barrel brewery in Teignmouth. We idled away an afternoon at the pub, half-sunk into huge-cushioned, wickerwork chairs outside on a day of mixed weather with a busy crowd and a few daring seagulls – happily the Steam Packet has a conservatory dining room by the terrace to which rained-on guests can scuttle, clutching their pints, if the heavens open.

The bar itself feels cosier, all dark wood and log fires; that's where we'd choose to perch in colder months, hands round a glass of the rich and mellow brown Jail Ale, made by the Dartmoor Brewery and available on draft here. A packet boat originally carried mail packets to British embassies and colonies; later the name simply meant a scheduled ship. We saw no larger ships this time, but the pub is clearly referencing its boaty setting at the estuary of the Dart river. It has four bedrooms above the bar which must prove popular with those seeking out the peaceful end of town during the Devon holiday season.

Beers and ciders are chalked up on a blackboard. We played with food matching, pairing Old Mills' Blonde Bombshell, a fruity pale barley malt, with crispy fried Brixham squid pieces dipped in delicious lime mayo, and loved a juicy, local Ashridge medium-dry cider with smoked haddock and chorizo fishcakes and a red pepper salsa.

Wines are not as inspiring as the beers and ciders, though they serve decent Provençal rosé, a snappy Picpoul de Pinet, and for those celebrating in style, both Taittinger and Laurent-Perrier from the grandes marques Champagne houses.

Desserts are notably good – Jude's Dairy ice creams and sorbets, a sublime, light, passionfruit bavarois and a richly flavoured, salted-caramel chocolate brownie. We dived indoors with them as the rain finally fell, finding not exactly a holistic retreat, but sanctuary in the conservatory bar.

Susy Atkins, 11 July 2015

St Peter's Quay, Totnes, Devon TQ9 5EW (01803 863880); steampacketinn.co.uk

The Masons Arms
Branscombe Village, Devon

It's thirsty work, the South West Coastal Path. Hours spent trudging into the wind on Portland, scrambling along Chesil Beach, fossicking at Lyme Regis, battling horsetails in the Lyme Undercliffs and trying to work out why they wrote the guidebook from west to east left us footsore and weary, beset by needs that only the frequent admixture of beer and salty snacks could assuage.

Many candidates for inclusion in this column suggested themselves: the Anchor in Beer was one, for obvious reasons. However, a rigorous application of Pint to Pint's exacting standards led to several deserving boozers (the Crown in Punchknowle – pron. 'Punnle' – and the Smugglers near Dawlish) being winnowed out in the qualifying rounds.

In the knockout stages, our selection criteria became more subjective. Dodgy typography disqualified one or two entries (the traditional Roman and Gothic signage of the country pub is under threat from modish sans-serif 'Keep Calm And Carry On'-type interlopers, while the judges felt the free-spirited nature of the West Country was too freely reflected by the use of Papyrus, a font better suited to a tanning salon in Essex than a half-timbered hostelry on the Devon–Dorset border).

More serious, and more difficult to arbitrate, was the perennial pub/restaurant issue. Many of these places draw most of their prosperity from food, and very nicely some of them do it, too. But where do you draw the line? At the Masons Arms, a thatched longhouse of unimpeachable prettiness a mile or so in from the coast, the answer is roughly halfway along the building.

Go left as you enter, and you're in a dining area that retains a certain pubby ambience (rough whitewashed walls, huge inglenook fireplace, brass rubbings over the bar, etc.) but where tables are set for eating delicious fresh fish and hearty pies, burgers and the like. To the right lies the 'Old Worthies Bar', a more authentically pub-like space (right down to the nacreous Turkish carpet), where, nevertheless, food is available.

Not being especially worthy, we sat in the food bit, but were delighted to find that the Masons is now owned by the St Austell Brewery, whose Proper Job, an aromatic and fruity beer, is on draught, alongside a plausible though not especially wide-ranging selection. It's a delicious and versatile pint and, despite its very West Country name, ought to be available more widely.

Too tired to see straight, we didn't get the most out of the Masons' chocolate-box beauty or rich historical hinterland (actual masons used to work here, dressing golden stone blocks for use on Exeter cathedral). But we did clock the circular thatch hats on tables outside, rustling in the spring breeze, imparting a vaguely, incongruously tropical air.

Keith Miller, 11 April 2015

Branscombe Village, Devon EX12 3DJ (01297 680300); masonsarms.co.uk

The Bell Inn
Watchet, Somerset

S tand outside The Bell Inn on the third Wednesday of each month and, if you shut your eyes, you could be back in the 18th century.

The salty tang of the sea air, the gentle lapping of the water against the hulls of moored ships, and from inside the tavern, the sound of ancient sea shanties accompanied by fiddle and mandolin.

All that's needed is the stomp of a peg-legged pirate, and you could imagine you were a character in the opening chapter of a swashbuckling *Treasure Island* adventure. Or at least an episode of *Captain Pugwash*.

Even the resident ales have nautical, pieces-of-eight names: there's doubloon-coloured Tribute (4.2%) from the St Austell Brewery in south Cornwall, first brewed to honour an eclipse of the sun; or there's Sharp's darker-hued Doom Bar, from Rock in north Cornwall, (4.0%), named after an infamous sandbank at the mouth of the Camel estuary.

It was in this waterside tavern that the poet Samuel Taylor Coleridge is said to have begun his epic poem *The Rime of the Ancient Mariner*, while walking in the Quantocks with William Wordsworth. These days, beer-drinking bards aren't perhaps as plentiful as they once were, but the inn's bookcases are positively awash with stories of old Watchet.

There are picture books showing the town as it used to be: Swain Street, the Cosy Cinema, the Esplanade, the old railway station (closed by Dr Beeching). Not to mention *The Illustrated Book of Fishes* and a set of *Reed's Nautical*

Almanacs dating back to the Seventies. There's even a poem paying tribute to the large number of pubs which once lay scattered hereabouts: 'A movement very soon begins/ Towards the ever-open inns./ The Greyhound, Ship, the Star as well;/ The Archer, London and The Bell.'

Not that more recent cultural events are overlooked: alongside the historic monochrome photographs on the wall, there's a framed copy of 'Something Is Happening' by Herman's Hermits.

Christopher Middleton, 12 October 2013

3 Market Street, Watchet, Somerset TA23 0AN (01984 631279); visit-watchet.co.uk/Members_Pages/Bell_Inn

The King Alfred
Burrowbridge, Somerset

O n the outdoor terrace at the back of the King Alfred,
a couple of local blokes, pints in hand, are watching
men and machines at work. You might be forgiven for
thinking that this is a case of the ale-drinking work-shy
watching the workers, but the contemplation of this duo is
more about remembrance.

At the start of the year, standing on the same terrace,
you'd have seen nothing but grey, rippling sheets of
flood water stretching out across the Somerset Levels.
Throughout the crisis the King Alfred acted as a
community centre for the surrounding farms and villages.

Now, on a benevolent autumn afternoon, the floods seem
far away apart from the chug-chug-chug of the diggers and
the presence of the sluggish River Parrett as it wends its
way to the sea. I nod to the two men and return to the bar
downstairs.

The contrast to the thoughtful situation outside couldn't
be any different. The bar is an elemental place of pews
and settles, hardy wooden tables and a tiled floor; it's lively
and noisy, roistering and rollicking as locals, walkers and
cyclists chat and caress their glasses of ale and cider.

Framed black-and-white photos of the pub throughout
the years line one wall, while the top gantry of the bar is
covered with hundreds of pump clips of past beers, a sign
that they take their drink seriously here. Live music is also
important; details of forthcoming gigs are chalked on a
solid wooden beam.

There's a family of eight in the window: three

generations, all tucking into their Yorkshires with gusto.

Meanwhile, at the bar, a middle-aged couple settle themselves on stools and discuss the renovation of a friend's waterlogged cottage. You can't get away from the floods that easily.

I catch the warm comforting waft of roast beef in the air as Sunday lunchtime continues on its merry way. The menu is a hearty digest that includes roast topside, home-reared lamb and Wessex free-range pork. From previous experience I know the portions are large. I'm not in the mood for food today, so I elect to sit at the bar and order a glass of Heck's cider.

'Which one?' asks the barmaid, pointing to a chalkboard with details of local ciders on offer. I am told that the one made with Brown's apples is crisp and tangy, while the Kingston Black variety is soft and slightly sweeter. I opt for the latter: it is smooth, full-bodied and has a dry finish. There are also three local cask beers, but the Heck's is delicious and having drained my glass I order another and muse on the pub's lively, likeable nature and raise a glass to its resilience.

The waters might have receded but this lunchtime crowd demonstrates that the pub's community spirit won't be forgotten in a rush.

Adrian Tierney-Jones, 18 October 2014

Burrow Drove, Burrowbridge, Bridgwater, Somerset TA7 0RB (01823 698379); king-alfred.co.uk

The Three Horseshoes Inn
Batcombe, Somerset

I t's an ironclad law of rural England that your best bet
for finding a pub in a strange village is to head for the
church. Beer-pump and pulpit share a long history and
Batcombe is no different: the stern and stately tower of St
Mary the Virgin overlooks the soft honey-coloured stone
of the four centuries-old Three Horseshoes with benign
paternalism.

Given that I passed a brace of boarded up pubs in
villages within several miles radius of Batcombe, you
might think The Three Horseshoes could do with divine
protection. Not so. The Almighty can rest easy. This gem of
a country pub is doing just fine.

The place looks warm and welcoming from the outside
and confirmation comes as you open the door. There's
an inglenook with an open fire on one side and a log-
burner on the other, making the place toasty. The décor is
restrained rustic with exposed stone walls, a low-beamed
ceiling and a smattering of prints.

Landlord Cav Javvi holds court at the bar, dispensing
drink and handing out menus with an easy manner. Beers
such as Butcombe Bitter and Bath Ales Gem tantalise on
the bar-top while local scrumpy and a pleasing selection of
wines offer a handsome alternative.

I plump for Wild Beer's Madness, lovingly crafted in
nearby Westcombe. It's an appetising India Pale Ale with
a Carmen Miranda hatful of tropical fruit on the nose
colliding passionately with a palate-zinging bitterness. It
is mouth-watering; the kind of beer that gets the digestive

juices going, which is just as well as The Three Horseshoes also majors in great grub.

I order the smoked chicken, game and leek terrine for starters, followed by a cheddar cheeseburger and skinny chips. The cheese is lush and unctuous as it drapes over the juicy burger. It's also made in Westcombe, one of only three cheddar cheese-makers to gain the Slow Food seal of approval.

The food style is robust British – great ingredients impeccably cooked. I watched people tuck into beer-battered fish and chips or chomp on a swirl of plump Cumberland sausage, nestled on a mountain of fluffy mash. Home-smoked haddock Florentine offered a lighter option. Local suppliers are used as much as possible, to the extent of reaching out to Batcombe's allotment addicts. A note on the wall declares: 'Allotment amnesty – if you have a surplus from your veg patches bring them in and swap for a pint or two.'

With its calm, unfussy décor and its almost evangelical passion for good food, The Three Horseshoes could so easily have become yet another gastro clone. Yet the pub welcomes all and pulls in the locals with its quiz nights and darts. All in all, it serves its congregation well – a cosy ambience, amiable company and good drink and food. Amen to that.

Adrian Tierney-Jones, 2 February 2013

Batcombe, Shepton Mallet, Somerset BA4 6HE (01749 850359); thethreehorseshoesinn.co.uk

The Plough Inn
Congresbury, Somerset

The Plough has flag floors, low-beamed ceilings and smells enticingly of wood smoke from several log fires. There are four or five small rooms, all more or less opened up to the bar – take your pick.

One haven celebrates today's Mendip Morris Men and their antecedents, with old photographs and a glass case with the full regalia of the Thirties: the hat, the baldrics, the bell pads and rosettes. Another small cosy corner by the bar tends to fill with older folk chin-resting on their walking sticks and putting the world to rights.

There's a room with its own bar window, but today is Wednesday and this evening there is a skittles match, so all the tables are reserved.

The pub is almost full, abuzz with conversation and laughter, and it's only 7.30pm. I hear a few cut glarse accents, some rolling Zummerzet burrs, and a lot in between; an ecumenical mix.

The visiting skittles team are called 'The Townies' and apparently they all drink lager. 'That's all right,' says Garry Polledri, the landlord, 'we've got a couple of lagers on tap, so they'll be happy enough. But this is a real ale pub.'

Indeed it is. There are half a dozen barrels at the back of the bar – the beers are served straight from the barrel. It's all south-western stuff. I spot St Austell's Tribute from Cornwall, Yeovil Brewery's Summerset, Palmer's Dorset Gold, Twisted Oak's Fallen Tree, and Butcombe's Bohemia. These last two breweries are in the same village, Wrington, just up the road.

A menu announces all sorts of seasonal goodies – game pie, pheasant and suchlike – but there are other names on the list that are hallowed to me, such as calves' liver, faggots, bubble and squeak, mushy peas, chips fried in beef fat.

I go for the faggots, which come with delicious onion gravy, chips, peas and a salad. It all sets me back £7.95 and there's so much on the plate that I can't finish it. Twisted Oak's Falling Tree, an amber beer at 3.8% with a surprising hop kick at the end, goes well with the meal.

Now to the skittles. This is the game played on a small table, with a ball on the end of a light chain. The skills on display are amazing – not just the players but also the scorers, who have to do the lightning maths on the chalkboard.

The chat, the jokes, the special lore and language of the game are wonderful. The beers flow. I try quite a few – they're all good. No notes, I'm afraid. Ho hum.

'What happens here in summer?' I ask. 'Ah,' says Garry, 'we have sixteen petanque teams who play out back – you should really come and see.' Do you know, I think I might just do that.

Arthur Taylor, 22 November 2014

High Street, Congresbury, Somerset BS49 5JA (01934 877402); the-plough-inn.net

The Orchard Inn
Bristol

H anging on the wall of The Orchard Inn is a photograph of the pub as it was in 1851: a small, unprepossessing, box-shaped building, the last in a terrace which ends rather abruptly.

It's the kind of place which might long ago have been bulldozed to the ground. Yet apart from the fact it used to be called The White Horse, the pub looks practically the same as it did 160 years ago.

The change of name is, however, significant. For what makes the Orchard stand out from its more comely counterparts is the fact that it serves not just one, not just two, but 23 different ciders.

Yes, there's no question what drink most appeals to the Orchard's core clientele. Just reading the chalked list is like taking a tour of the West Country, each with its own potted biography, plus wooziness rating (between 6% and 7% ABV).

There are board games in the bookcase (Monopoly, Mid-Life Crisis, Trivial Pursuit), and cheery characters at the bar; among them, white-bearded Mick the Boat.

'Have the Surfin' Turnips,' he suggests. 'That's my favourite cider.'

'Pay no attention,' says Des the barmaid. 'Have what you like.'

And that turns out to be four half-pints, hand-picked by Des for a cross-section of flavours. The Ashridge (from Totnes) comes out top of the tree in terms of sheer amplified appleyness; but it is just pipped by the Black

Dragon (from Wales), so rich and full-flavoured, it dips a clawed toe into the realms of sherry.

There's no steamed sea bass on the menu, but there are three types of roll on the counter: ham salad, cheese salad, Stilton and red onion. Plus a free plate of toasted French bread and hot beef dripping.

'Help yourself,' says Des, while Mick (he lives in the next-door marina) tells the tale of the Japanese girl who tried to drink her way from top to bottom of the cider list.

'Got more than half way, she did,' he says approvingly. 'She didn't exactly pass out, just subsided gracefully onto the floor. We helped her friends carry her back to Legoland.'

Which is how the locals refer to the new apartments going up in this Harbourside part of town. Not that there's any antipathy towards the newcomers. At weekends, boatfolk and flat-dwellers mix with the crowd from the Spike Island arts centre, cider oiling the shoulder-rubbing.

That the pub's roots go deep into the community is borne out by the busy blackboards, announcing everything from jazz nights to forthcoming ciders to quiz nights (£1 per person, winner takes all).

And of course, there are always new ciders to try. Even when you've had four, there are still nineteen to go.

Christopher Middleton, 18 May 2013

Hanover Place, Harbourside, Bristol BS1 6XT;
theorchardinn.co.uk

The Salamander
Bath

E ven though Bath is usually associated with Jane Austen,
the author who springs to mind on first discovering
The Salamander is Thomas Hardy. *Far From the Madding
Crowd* to be precise, as it's hidden away down a sparsely
populated road off the properly peaceful Quiet Street.
You're more likely to discover locals, office workers and the
odd phalanx of rugby fans here than hordes of camera-
clicking tourists.

Those holidaymakers are missing a treat. The
Salamander is a gorgeous Georgian building, set in the
obligatory honeyed limestone terrace, facing the world
through a wide bay window hung with flower baskets.

Inside there are three distinct areas. In the front you can
sip your pint overlooking the street and spy on folk going
about their business. A collection of games piled high in
an old fireplace offers extra distraction. Farther in, past
the bar, there's a den-like area in which to practise the
philosophy of the pub, the Tao of the tap room, the Path of
the Pint, etc. – to have a quiet beer or three, in other words.

As for the décor, it's a mix of pared down, artfully
distressed wooden floorboards and minimalist cream-
coloured walls – though a framed Bath rugby shirt signed
by erstwhile local legend Stuart Barnes adds a worldly note.
The bar is imposing and sturdy, backed by mahogany brown
shelves and alcoves, all comfortingly packed with wine and
beer bottles. This is a solid pub, rooted to the earth.

The 'Sal' has been owned by Bath Ales brewery for
ten years (the barman lets slip that it had a 'reputation'

previously), and four of its cask beers are on show. What to choose? Stuart Barnes pops up again, this time in beer form (the transmigration of souls – must be all that philosophy). I order a glass of Barnsey and repose on a bar stool. Good call. It's a stocky chestnut-coloured ale of 4.5% ABV, pumped up with chocolate and toffee notes and a dry, roasty character in the background. A rugby player's pint indeed.

The menu is similarly robust: black pudding croquettes, cheeseburgers, sticky red wine pork belly. The pie of the day is shin of beef cooked in Bath's Dark Side stout – my mind is made up.

This is a rich concoction of meaty juice and crisp pastry, one of the best pies I've had in a long time. And as I eat I'm accompanied by the quiet murmur of conversation from a scattering of drinkers, while a couple sit in the window reliving their youth with a giggly game of draughts. As time passes, knowledgeable locals and one or two particularly intrepid tourists drift in, and the pub slowly wakes up from its mid-afternoon siesta.

The Salamander is, to use the name of one of Bath Ales' other beers, a Gem, offering relaxation, people-watching, civilised conversation and highly accomplished food and drink. Just don't tell the madding crowd.

Adrian Tierney-Jones, 11 January 2014

John Street, Bath BA1 2JL (01225 428889); www.bathales.com/salamander

The Ebrington Arms
Chipping Campden, Gloucestershire

O n approach this looks like a tiny inn, but the
Ebrington Arms is bigger than it appears – much
wider than it looks from outside, with four large rooms
running the length of the 17th-century building.

The bar itself is small enough to look packed even if it's
not a full house. The owners, Claire and Jim Alexander,
have chosen their staff incredibly, so service is efficient and
friendly and any waiting is brief. A small fireplace makes
for a cosy winter pint and locals appreciate a pub that's 'not
snobby', where you can wear your boots and bring your dog
– the joy of flagstone floors.

I pull up a bar stool and sample a pint of the pub's own
Yubby Bitter (3.8%). This, and a brown ale called Yawnie,
are brewed at the nearby North Cotswold Brewery but the
beers' recipes are created by pub staff. There are usually
four additional cask ales to choose from, most from the
local area.

A modest £3.50 gets you a beer 'tasting flight' of three
thirds of a pint, a concept imported from craft brew bars
in the United States but growing in popularity in the UK.
Despite this North American influence Yubby is made
exclusively with British hops and was designed to have
a flavour somewhere between Flowers IPA and Fuller's
London Pride, an excellent example of a classic British
session beer.

In the next room a fantastic – but nevertheless stuffed –
fox jumps up at you as you enter a magnificent space that
was once a bakery but is now dominated by huge barrel-

shaped settles next to a Tudor-style fireplace.

A small flight of stairs takes you down to the pub's former kitchen and on to another dining area overlooking the garden from which, in warmer weather, Cotswold scenery can be enjoyed.

Relics such as a butcher's hook in the ceiling add to the historic atmosphere of the pub and hint at a certain robustness in the cuisine.

Free range pork belly with pheasant sausage, black cabbage and a pheasant consommé (£17), for example, proves a meaty delight and easily demonstrates why the Ebrington has two AA rosettes for its food. Starters are priced from £6.50; mains cost from £13 to £24. Ingredients are mostly locally sourced and seasonal – witness the quince jelly made from fruit from one of the locals' gardens.

There have been lively episodes here in the past, such as the Christmas Eve Fracas of 1932, a near-riot triggered by locals trying to stop drunken carol singing by pub patrons. Further back still, the first landlord – in 1717 – was done for keeping a disorderly alehouse and subsequently lost his licence. These days things may get busy – with good reason – but the best of order prevails.

Sophie Atherton, 25 January 2014

Ebrington, Chipping Campden, Gloucestershire GL55 6NH (01386 593223); theebringtonarms.co.uk; open from 9am daily

South-East England

The General Eliott
South Hinksey, Oxfordshire

Oxford blues? No more: the village of South Hinksey has its pub back. Located within sight of the university's dreaming spires, the village is gripped in the Tarmac embrace of the city's roaring ring road.

Some six years ago, something within the village died when its pub closed. South Hinksey's identity and independence all seemed under threat. The village, like the narrow, quiet road leading to it off the A34, was seemingly going nowhere. For five years the pub, which had won many plaudits for the quality of its beers and welcome, stood empty and silent. The windows were boarded and the grass in the beer garden grew long.

But villagers didn't give up the thought that one day it would return – they socialised in each other's houses, fought plans to have the pub's site redeveloped as houses and dreamt of the day when their local would reopen.

Then, in 2013, two villagers, Cass and Helen Hazlewood, bought the derelict General Eliott and began the long process of resuscitation; it reopened last autumn. Now, once more it's a thriving country pub. Inside, staff behind the L-shaped bar are warm and welcoming, and you get the feeling that it doesn't matter how many want to come inside, room will always be found for one more.

One of the pub's donnish customers tells me the village's name is Anglo-Saxon and means either Hengist's Island or Stallion's Island. As for General Eliott, that redoubtable hero of the Siege of Gibraltar allegedly popped his clogs after a surfeit of mineral water – a lesson for us all, there.

It's clear that water is still an issue hereabouts (one couple, sitting by one of the pub's welcoming open fires, talk about much-needed flood prevention plans). And horses still feature in village life, as riders canter down from the Old Manor Riding School in North Hinksey for a cheeky prosecco.

It's not just fizz, or a wide range of local beers, that is proving popular: a group of mountain bike riders are tucking into pints of prawns served with fresh bread and large bowls of garlic mayonnaise. Blackboards describe the daily menu: contemporary comfort food – wholesome steaks, ham and chips. A family, who have made the 25-minute walk from Oxford's city centre, choose a large platter of meat and cheese for sharing. Outside, children chatter in the garden and point at the red kite circling overhead.

Another group have walked from Happy Valley, now a nature park, on the other side of the ring road. There they strolled in the footsteps of Victorian poet Matthew Arnold, and the great Oxford watercolourist William Turner (not to be confused with the more celebrated J.M.W.). Today's walkers, though, use apps, not watercolours or notebooks, to record their memories.

Tim Hampson, 9 May 2015

Manor Road, South Hinksey, Oxfordshire OX1 5AS (01865 608567); thege.co.uk

The Bear Inn
Oxford

The first thing you'll notice on entering the Bear are the ties; clippings of ties to be accurate, assembled in serried ranks and placed in glass showcases that cover the walls and the ceiling. They're not any old ties either. The owners of these ties were members of famed colleges, schools, regiments, sports clubs and long lost establishments such as the Palestine Police. The donations started in the Fifties and still continue, though the practice of a drink on the house for the clip of a tie is sadly no longer observed.

However there's more to this classic city pub than being an upmarket Tie Rack for boozers. It's been around since the 1500s (some claim it to be older), a longevity that gives it an air of great venerability. The floor is oak, worn and weathered by the feet of countless generations, while the light chestnut-brown tones of the wooden panelling are warm and comforting; both the snug and side bar have that indefinable sense of cosiness that makes for a great pub (there's also a back room with more ties).

When I enter, it's early evening and the place is humming with conversation – this being Oxford you get a higher standard of pub chat. Around me I pick up threads of discussions on the conductivity of various metals, Vichy France and Association Football in the 19th century. This is the pub as a place of learning (although the regulars in the snug are gossiping about one-time Oxford resident Robert Maxwell).

There's also plenty of good beer as it's owned by the

exemplary Fuller, Smith & Turner. There are six beers on the bar and I opt for the mighty ESB with its Cointreau-orange character contrasting with an appetisingly grainy dryness and rolling thunder of bitterness.

As I dedicate myself to it, I also note a warm gravy-like aroma in the air, no doubt coming from the kitchen, which reminds me it's time to eat. The menu is a fine example of brawny pub grub including steak and ale pie, lamb shank, and salmon and dill fish cakes. Another swig of my beer and I decide to choose the steak and ale pie, which turns out to be a juicy, meaty feast. Outside in the evening glow, bicyclists and pedestrians whirr and amble past. Poor them. I order another ESB.

Given the nature of Oxford, the Bear could so easily have become a tatty tourist trap, but this is an inn that has adapted to changing times while still retaining a sense of its ancient charm. It has rooted itself in the centre of Oxford like a great sturdy tree, and given the transient nature of many of those that pass through its doors maybe that's its strength. Being a home from home to both regulars and strangers has helped it to survive and prosper through the ages.

Adrian Tierney-Jones, 29 March 2014

6 Alfred Street, Oxford OX1 4EH (01865 728164);
bearoxford.co.uk

The Wellington Arms
Baughurst, Hampshire

Set in three acres on the outskirts of Baughurst village, The Wellington Arms keeps a small flock of Jacob sheep and Tamworth pigs, which happily graze the lush paddock and rootle among the beech trees. Beehives and fruit trees are dotted around a sizeable kitchen garden.

Given the flock of gleaming Range Rover Evoques in the manicured car park, I assumed the picturebook farm animals were for light petting duties only. But no, they're on the menu, having numbers rather than names to avoid any awkward attachments. The rescue chickens get off lightly, donating only their eggs to make first-class 'rescue custard'.

There's a touch of *The Good Life* about the almost-self-sufficient idyll that chef Jason King and former classical music teacher Simon Page have created on the edge of the North Hampshire Downs.

Before they bought the place in 2005 it was an old-school boozer called The New Inn, popular with rugby players and fans. Its new name reflects its former life as a hunting lodge on the Duke of Wellington's Stratfield Saye estate.

The Welly, as the new regulars call it, is now a full-on dining pub. There are two real ales on tap, the dependable Wadworth's 6X (4.1%) and perfumed Cavalier Golden Ale (3.8%) from the nearby Two Cocks brewery, but the drinks on the blackboard, Aperol Spritz and Negroni, reflect the casually sophisticated tone. The fine wine list features sparkling wines from the local Coates & Seely winery.

The bar feels a bit like the counter in a village shop, selling eggs, pub-made jams and retro tea cosies knitted by Simon's mother. Sloe gin is served from a crystal decanter. The low-beamed, bijoux dining area seats around 40, including Judith Chalmers on our visit.

Logs are stacked beside the brick fireplace, and dogs are welcome. Ours was presented with water and a biscuit, unbidden (and, no, they didn't know I was writing a review).

Jason does his produce extremely proud, cooking up top-drawer country classics with a seasonal gamey twist. The Welly's fat chips are hand-cut, and he makes a mean ham-hock terrine. From the Simple Lunch menu (two courses £16, three for £19) we scoffed a brace of barrage-balloon bangers with velvety mash, caramelised onions and a jug of red-wine sauce; and 'proper' cottage pie with actual pieces of beef and pork.

The kitchen garden is reminiscent of Mr McGregor's vegetable patch but, in this version of events, Peter Rabbit is braised with cavolo nero, fennel and a piquant mustard sauce.

Jonathan Goodall, 29 November 2014

Baughurst Road, Baughurst, Hampshire RG26 5LP (0118 982 0110); thewellingtonarms.com

The Willow Tree
Winchester

G iven that you don't find many pubs on islands, The Willow Tree comes as a surprise. It stands on not one, but two.

Admittedly, the first is a traffic island. More appealingly, though, the building is surrounded by water. One branch of the River Itchen goes right underneath the pub, while another sneaks up round the side. Effectively turning The Willow Tree's back garden into a triangle, besieged on both sides by a rushing stream.

All the more surprising, then, that despite being under assault from the combined forces of nature and the combustion engine, The Willow Tree somehow remains a place of calm. It helps, of course, that on one side it has an attractive array of back gardens, and, on the other, a row of brick cottages that could come straight out of a Jane Austen novel.

As for the pub itself, it is divided into pub (left-hand side) and restaurant (right). There is no mistaking the ranks of shiny cutlery laid out on the tables in the dining area. They serve as a pointed challenge to anyone who is contemplating coming in and having a quick half of bitter, as opposed to a £13 fish stew or £18 rib-eye steak.

Instead, those seeking a snack are drawn to the left-hand side of the building. Here, a blackboard lists the less filling food, casually dispensing both with the pound signs and the zeros in the pence column. Thus, chips cost 3, cheesy chips cost 4, and lovely, warm, Scotch egg a delicious 2.5.

Even more of a nose-thumbing to traditional pub ways, is the fact that the beers are all temporary guests, rather than feet-under-the-table regulars.

In order to commend themselves to drinkers, then, each beer comes with its own catchphrase. The ruby-hued Colonel's Whiskers (4.3% ABV, from Batemans) is depicted by a bristly moustache and the legend 'Nose Tickling Beer'. Meanwhile, the Autumn Stout (5% ABV, from St Peter's Brewery, in Suffolk) opts less for whimsy and more for hard fact, with its motto 'Strong and Dark'.

Both are for people who like their drinks dusky and dry. The only lighter-coloured ale on offer on this particular day is Goddards' Scrum Diggity (4% ABV), billed as 'Isle of Wight Born and Brewed'.

As for the Willow Tree soundtrack, it's mellow jazz inside the pub, and up-tempo splashing outside. The water flows under and around the pub in distinctly preoccupied fashion, as if it has an urgent appointment somewhere out of town.

All the better, then, to position yourself at one of the outdoor tables, and let the river propel its sticks and leaves onwards. After all, as everyone knows, there is nothing more relaxing than sitting with a glass of beer and watching the rest of the world rush by.

Christopher Middleton, 27 December 2014

14 Durngate Terrace, Winchester, Hampshire SO23 8QX (01962 877255); thewillowtreewinchester.co.uk

The Jolly Sailor
Old Bursledon, Hampshire

There are two ways to arrive at the Jolly Sailor in the village of Bursledon: via steep stone steps down the back of the pub, or by pontoon across the water to the front. With a ship's figurehead in the form of a – yes – jolly sailor poised above the door to the river frontage, we wondered if those arriving by water would be given a warmer welcome than those who came by Shanks' pony.

It was a pretty daft way of thinking.

We may not have been in the 'yellow welly brigade' – we had no oilskins or dungarees – but inside, we felt as immediately relaxed and happy as the ruddy-faced boat people around us.

With pints of Badger First Gold and a lushly-filled Stargazy pie – nestling in an old-school ashet, and topped with light, flaky pastry – we breathed a sigh of contented afternoon delight.

For years the Jolly Sailor was the local boozer in the BBC serial Howard's Way, all Eighties hair and shoulder pads, set along the gin-and-Jag belt of the Solent coast. A framed picture of the bouffanted cast takes pride of place on one of the walls. Some Jolly punters come on a pilgrimage to the show; but most come for the beer, the view, the pies – or just because their yacht is outside in Swanwick Marina.

The Jolly Sailor sits right on the edge of the River Hamble, and its beer gardens spread themselves across stepped terraces, decks and pontoons – there are covered nooks and crannies, such as 'The Cabin' where a sign warns you to 'mind your head'.

The building was originally a vicarage, but has been a pub since 1845. Low-beamed ceilings, ships' lanterns, and naval paraphernalia add to the distressed but tasteful seafaring-themed comfort of the place. One wall quotes Leonardo da Vinci: 'He who loves practice without theory is like a sailor who boards a ship without a rudder and compass, and never knows where he may cast.'

A bucket filled with apples has a note urging people to help themselves and keep the doctor away. And a wooden seat is marked 'Bunter's Bench' – this being the childhood nickname given to the brother of the chairman of Hall and Woodhouse, the brewery that owns the pub. There are two regular Hall and Woodhouse pump ales: Badger First Gold, a bitter with a note of both oranges and spice, and Tangle Foot. A seasonal guest ale changes every three months – currently it is Hopping Hare, with a summery citrus taste. On a previous, wintry visit, it was Firkin Fox, a biscuity auburn ale.

Returning to the car, parked in the nearby Bursledon station car park, we couldn't help wishing we were the ones in the yellow wellies – for then we could spend all day here at the Jolly Sailor, and be no more than a pontoon's reach from a comfy bunk. That would surely be the best way?

Audrey Gillan, 31 August 2013

Land's End Road, Old Bursledon, Hampshire SO31 8DN (023 8040 5557); jollysaileroldbursledon.co.uk

The Bat and Ball
Clanfield and Hambledon, Hampshire

The taxi driver sounds almost apologetic as he drops me outside the Bat and Ball and pockets eighteen quid for the journey from Petersfield station. 'Not much here,' he says. No bus stops. No cricketers either on a midweek lunchtime when the hallowed turf of Broadhalfpenny Down is left to the moles.

It will be different at the weekend when either the Brigands CC or Hambledon thirds are at home. Hambledon first and second elevens now play in a similarly sublime setting a mile or so down the road. But it was here that the club played an All England XI on 51 occasions between 1750 and 1787, winning no fewer than 29 times.

Their captain was Richard Nyren, landlord of the Bat and Ball. His son John wrote *The Cricketers of My Time*, illuminating the likes of Edward 'Lumpy' Stevens, whose deadly underarm 'shooters' took a terrible toll on pad-less shins, and William 'Silver Billy' Beldham wielding his bat with 'a wrist that seemed to turn on springs of the finest steel'. Substantial crowds drank barleycorn ale that 'flared like turpentine' at 2d a pint.

The Fuller's London Pride in the Bat and Ball today is more expensive at £3.70. It doesn't flare like turpentine, but it sharpens taste buds for a menu on which locally reared steak and bacon feature. Game, too, in season.

The local gamekeeper, David Mann, is sitting at the bar, nursing a well-earned pint of Gales HSB, brewed in Chiswick rather than Horndean these days. He has been up since dawn nurturing the chicks destined to grow into targets for the shooting parties that will begin descending on the pub as the cricket season draws to a close.

Cricketing history is chronicled on the walls, particularly on that side of the pub officially in Hambledon rather than Clanfield. White lines mark the boundary, a legacy of the days when they came under different licensing authorities and you had to move from one to the other if you wanted to carry on drinking legally.

No such constraints these days. I can lingeringly savour the Gales Spring Sprinter, an astringent palate-cleanser with hints of gooseberry, while checking off the attributes of the classic country pub: weathered beams, horse-brasses around open fireplaces, leather settles, pewter tankards over the bar – and stunning views.

None more stunning than the vista of Broadhalfpenny Down where the ghosts of Lumpy Stevens and Silver Billy are all too easy to imagine. Whatever the taxi driver says, there's plenty here for those of us who love cricket as well as beer.

Chris Arnot, 25 April 2015

Hyden Farm Lane, Clanfield, Waterlooville, Hampshire PO8 0UB (02392 632692); batandballclanfield.co.uk

The Three Horseshoes

Thursley, Surrey

When you hear about village communities rallying around to save their pub, you think of hard-pressed volunteers, rotas and shoestring budgets.

That's not quite the story of The Three Horseshoes. It may have been rescued from closure by the good people of Thursley, but by no stretch of the imagination are they impoverished ploughfolk. Come here on a weekend lunchtime, and you will be looking not at pickled onions and a slab of cheddar, but confit of duck leg (£16.50) and fillet of sea bass (£20).

For this is the prosperous, leafy heart of Surrey. Is that the veteran broadcaster Alan Whicker, sitting at the bar, doing the crossword? Why, I think it is. And is this pretty pink mansion (Street House) the place where Sir Edwin Lutyens was brought up, and that, just across the road, the first house that he designed (The Corner)? Again, the answer is yes.

Speaking of architecture, the interior of the pub has been skilfully scooped out to provide the maximum amount both of dining space and quirky corners. Tables turn up in all kinds of unexpected alcoves and alleyways, but even in the more informal front bar, they bear the knife-fork-and-napkin that says 'If you're going to sit here, we expect you to eat'.

You get the feeling here that regulars know the ropes, while stray ramblers have stumbled into uncharted territory, unaware that for a weekend lunch at The Three Horseshoes, you need to book a table in advance.

Not that it's a disaster if you don't, thanks to the lovely, big garden out at the back, with views over ploughed fields, picture book cottages and a pretty little church.

Even the A3 is reduced from growling monster to distant landmark, with only the faint swish of engines audible above the birdsong.

Few pub views are prettier than this, especially when viewed across an expanse of deliciously fruity TEA (Traditional English Ale, 4.2% ABV, from the nearby Hog's Back Brewery) or coppery Hophead (3.8%, from Dark Star, of West Sussex).

After which, you'll be ready for a walk through the village, which is like strolling through the pages of a glossy country magazine. Alternatively, you can pick up a walks leaflet in the pub, which will guide you through the next-door nature reserve and steer you towards a disused 17th-century iron forge or the grave of a murdered 18th-century sailor.

One route even takes you to a platform where you can peer inside the Hindhead road tunnel, before you return to the village, via stiles and running streams. Yes, this may be the countryside, but it's not so much red in tooth and claw, as green and pleasant, and knows its place.

Christopher Middleton, 15 June 2013

Dye House Road, Thursley, Surrey GU8 6QD (01252 703268); threehorseshoesthursley.com

The Grantley Arms
Wonersh, Surrey

It's sometimes hard to remember that there are two Surreys. One is the province of mansion-dwelling Chelsea footballers and gleaming 4WD monsters. The other is an altogether rougher-edged county, with hills and forests and ancient, weatherboarded barns.

Take the village of Wonersh, which is just six miles from Guildford, yet its main street consists of a few half-timbered houses and a cobbled pavement. There is one shop, one pedestrian shelter, and one pub.

This is the Grantley Arms, named after the erstwhile Lord Grantley, a man so at ease with the common folk that he required the walls around his estate to be high enough to stop the peasants peeking in.

Like most structures in Wonersh, the pub (built in the 17th century) scorns the use of right angles, preferring to go for slopes and slants, and ceilings that are held up by wooden supports.

It's short on walls, too. Instead of different rooms, there are different areas: a library area here, a fireplace area there, a railway carriage-like area there. And, just the other side of a curtain, a beautifully preserved skittle alley (hire charge £14.50 per person).

Beer-wise, the pub serves a large range, all listed on the blackboard with ale colour helpfully appended. Thus the local Surrey bitter (from Pilgrim, 3.7% ABV) is 'bronze', the MGA (Cottage Brewery, Somerset, 4% ABV) is 'golden', and the Itchen Valley Winchester (4.5% ABV) is 'mid-brown'. And just a deliciously bit sweet.

Food is more sons-of-the-soil than lord-of-the-manor; the lunch menu includes several variations on the theme of egg and chips priced in the £7–£9 bracket, plus any number of differently filled ciabattas (or 'ciabatters', endearingly) with chips for £6.50. Apple pie and banana split (both £4.95) fill any gaps that are left.

That's not to say the Grantley Arms caters only for the muddy-booted. There are smarter evening meals on the menu (whitebait, steaks, lamb shanks etc., starters from £4.75, mains from around £10), and a lengthy wine list to go with them. There can't be many pubs that offer their customers a choice between an all-day breakfast (£8.95) and a bottle of Bollinger (£55).

Yes, we may have our class differences in this country, but we resolve them not by use of the guillotine, but by providing a range of dishes to suit all tastes and pockets. It makes you feel proud to be British.

Not as proud, though, as when you visit the parkland next to the village church. Once the private domain of Lord Grantley, this green was bought up by a determined local lady, one Mrs Beatrice Cook, who promptly donated it 'for the quiet use of residents of Wonersh. In perpetuity.'

Now that's revolution, British-style.

Christopher Middleton, 14 December 2013

The Street, Wonersh, Guildford, Surrey GU5 0PE (01483 893351); thegrantleyarms.co.uk

The Halfway Bridge
Lodsworth, West Sussex

The concept of the coaching inn is genius. You break your journey, rest, eat and drink – and then and only then, after you've enjoyed the best hospitality said hostelry can offer, climb into another coach to be driven off on the next leg.

The fine 17th-century coaching inn that is The Halfway Bridge was owned by the now-defunct Horsham-based King and Barnes Brewery but is now in independent hands. Perched on the A272 between Petworth and Midhurst, if the pub has an eventful history, it's not shouting about it, although the road features in a Monty Python sketch about Picasso painting a picture while taking part in a cycling race ('this is … the first time that a modern artist of such stature has taken the A272').

The pub's interior is labyrinthine, with many rooms in which to eat or drink, all of which have their own individual feel – The Halfway Bridge is well placed to be all things to all people. Solid wood tables in one room are somewhat rustically distressed: despite the classy leather chairs and contemporary place settings, these conjure an image of buxom barmaids trying to keep bawdy patrons in check and a trio of highwaymen in the corner, plotting their next raid.

The feel and sight of a plush rug beneath my feet brought me back to the present. I calmed my wild imagination with a half-pint of the appropriately named Halfway to Heaven, a 3.5% malty session ale with a light floral flavour and a hint of hops in the finish, from nearby

Langham Brewery who make it especially for the pub. Their punchier Hip Hop and Sharp's Doom Bar are also served.

In another room, a huge fireplace contains a small wood-burning stove but also a magnificent triple-panelled back plate. A sizeable pile of logs tells you how cosy The Halfway Bridge would be on a cold day. Not that this saved the pub from the scourge of last winter's storms and ensuing power cuts – which threatened to scupper festivities from Christmas Eve until Boxing Day. The friendly and super-capable Canadian bartender Joy explained to me how they moved as many bookings as they could to sister pub the Crab & Lobster in Sidlesham, and offered everyone else a free meal in compensation.

Although I was making use of the inn in the traditional sense of breaking my journey, I didn't have a coachman to help me with the next bit – and I didn't have time to try the food. It looked hearty and ambitious, if a little expensive (£28 for fillet steak). But if it's anything like the fare at the aforementioned Crab & Lobster, it'll be worth the money.

Bring on the age of driverless cars – or a return to the glory days of the coaching inn. If they are all as good as this, I feel a UK tour coming on …

Sophie Atherton, 20 September 2014

Lodsworth, Petworth, West Sussex GU28 9BP (01798 861281); halfwaybridge.co.uk

The North Laine Brewhouse
Brighton

A friendly young woman at the bar has just offered me one of her wasabi-coated cashew nuts with the warning: 'They're a bit spicy.' She's not kidding. My mouth is not so much tingling as smouldering and I'm wondering whether the IPA that I've just ordered can compete with powerful Japanese horseradish.

Compete? The wasabi is simply steamrollered. This pale ale has recoated the tongue with a satisfyingly dry and uncompromisingly bitter aftertaste. It's a bold beer, 5% alcohol by volume, characteristic of the new brews emerging from across the Atlantic. American hops, American malt. And the brewer is called Dallas.

Yet Nigel Dallas works right here in Brighton, England.* You can watch him work on a platform behind the bar where a gleaming line of huge silver vats contribute to a décor best described as light-industrial – stripped brick, grey tiles and long benches made from recycled floorboards.

The North Laine has been created in the sizeable shell of a former nightclub on the edge of the district of the same name, a network of narrow streets lined with cafés, bars and oddball shops that define the new, anything-goes Brighton.

While the pub feels in some ways like a beer hall, the use of many candles bestows a more mellow intimacy on the surroundings. They're glowing not just on the benches but also on the wooden barrels used to rest drinks on. The barrels are opened up in the middle, providing storage for the shoulder bags that appear to be de rigueur for both sexes among a youthful clientele this Friday evening.

Craft beer has become cool, metaphorically speaking. Hooker (4%) is just the right temperature for an amber ale, though Nigel confides that it's still a work in progress. 'We brought it in as a session beer for the Six Nations rugby, but it needs tweaking a bit.' A rich stout and a porter are available at various times, occasionally at a discount from the standard £3.70 or £3.80 a pint.

On Saturday lunchtime the atmosphere is more family-friendly. Food includes a 'pie of the day' and gammon with duck egg. My wife's fish and chips live up to the seaside location. The fish is white and flaky, the beery batter light and crisp. My pile of mussels comes with chunks of warm bread. Having dipped one in the creamy sauce, my food-scientist daughter pronounces it 'quite bitter'.

'That's because the mussels have been cooked in IPA,' I say.

'IPA?'

'Mmmm. Don't mind if I do.'

Chris Arnot, 9 March 2013

---

*Nigel Dallas is no longer the brewer at The North Laine. Nic Donald is now head brewer.

---

27 Gloucester Place, Brighton BN1 4AA (01273 683666); brewedinbrighton.co.uk; food served noon–9.30pm Mon–Fri, noon–8pm weekends

The Snowdrop Inn
Lewes, East Sussex

There's a beautiful chalk cliff behind the Snowdrop, innocuous and innocent, stitched with greenery, a memorable and camera-friendly backdrop. Appearances can be deceptive, though, especially for those people who would have been sitting in the houses that stood on this street in 1836. Heavy snow had fallen and was piled up on the cliff like one of those Georgian ladies' wigs that were just slipping out of fashion. On 27 December the snow put Newton's law of gravity into effect and the worst British avalanche occurred, killing at least eight people. When all the debris was cleared, the Snowdrop was built.

On the summer's evening I visited, the prospect of an avalanche was about as unlikely as the Guido Fawkes Society canvassing for members in bonfire-crazy Lewes. I stepped into a cheerfully decorated space with an island bar at its centre. It had the feel of a massive wooden cabin, though my drinking companion suggested that it was more reminiscent of the jumbled innards of those houseboats that drift along the old canals of England.

There was the usual assembly of pub knick-knacks scattered about, all done in the most tasteful way. There was history and music: one wall featured framed black-and-white photos of the area, alongside ancient handbills for entertainers as diverse as Max Miller and the Rolling Stones. There was oddness: some puppets lounged on a shelf. Then there was charity: next to the piano, a life-size collection box for guide dogs featured a fibreglass yellow Labrador with a couple of cute pups at its feet.

The mood of the pub was warm and friendly; the voices of the early crowd a sine wave of conversation. One couple discussed what they were going to eat, while another, perhaps unaware of the pub's history, gently argued about the best time to go snowboarding. An Irish wolfhound stood still next to a table as its owner polished off a pint – the lot of the pubgoer's pooch is a patient one.

The pub prides itself on its beer. I ordered a glass of Saison from local brewery Burning Sky, which was tart and refreshing and speared through with lemon, peppery notes. It was the perfect beer for a warm evening, though I also had my eye on Harvey's superlative Best Bitter, which is only brewed about five minutes away.

The pub prides itself on its food and is keen on seasonal and locally sourced products. The menu included local charcuterie, rabbit and freshly caught fish, but I went for the succulent, delicately spiced home-made scotch egg (I was in a pub after all).

Meanwhile, voices hummed and whirred as the evening grew, interspersed with the clink of glasses and sudden eruptions of laughter. It would have taken an avalanche to make me leave.

Adrian Tierney-Jones, 23 August 2014

119 South Street, Lewes, East Sussex BN7 2BU (01273 471018); thesnowdropinn.com

The Crown Inn
Hastings, East Sussex

Sunshine is dancing through the windows, bringing a lovely glow into what is really quite a dark room – all black and navy paint, beamed ceilings and old wood. But the Crown is not the least bit broody or sullen. Not with red vaudeville-style lights running behind the bar and paintings on the walls.

This is a traditional old boozer given a big lick of paint and a lot of love, and since it opened a year ago it has stolen the hearts not just of the hip, arty FILTH 'Failed In London Try Hastings' crowd, but also the old-school stalwarts: the hippies, the fishermen and a host of other characters who call this seaside town home.

Just below the East Hill country park and a pebble's throw from the stony beach, the Crown sits on All Saints Street; its pavement tables and chairs overlook a terraced row of higgledy-piggledy houses. (Some of the oldest surviving buildings in Hastings – dating from 1450 – are in this street.) There are dogs inside and out, people playing board games or snoozing in the corner. It is high summer when we visit, and there are wild flowers on the tables. In less clement weather there are log fires and it wouldn't surprise me if the bar staff brought out knee blankets.

The Crown lay empty for a few years until it was spotted by Tess Eaton and Andrew Swan, a young couple who had moved down from Leeds with a plan to change the ambience of the place, with a little help from the area's rich seam of craftsmen and producers – the vast crown sculpture above the door, the furniture, the art, the illustrations are all by locals.

The theme continues on the pumps, where the rotating selection will always include ales and beer from Sussex. There's straw-coloured, earthy but citrusy Hastings Beer's Saison Simple (4% ABV) from nearby St Leonards as well as their 3Cs American Pale Ale. English Garden Ale (3.8%), is from Franklins Brewery in Bexhill.

There's a whole host of stuff from outside Sussex, including St Michael's Bitter (4%) from the Cornish Crown Brewery and Black IPA (5.9%) from TicketyBrew in Stalybridge. There are nineteen ciders available, mostly by the bottle, and an amazing selection of gins (twelve of them) and whiskeys (sixteen).

With fishing boats landing their catch directly on Hastings beach, and smokeries abounding, the Crown's menu really makes the best of the local larder – skate wing, mussels, peas, peashoots, leeks and seafood cream followed by strawberries, shortbread, vanilla cream and lemon meringue ice cream from nearby Bodiam.

And in its bid to truly embrace localism, the Crown hosts regular events including a crafting bee – think macramé potholder-weaving and leather coin-purse-making – and 'Sunday stories in the snug'; there's a pub quiz, occasional music and odd sessions such as wild foraging followed by cocktail-making and brewery tap takeovers. I wish it was my local.

Audrey Gillan, 29 August 2015

64–66 All Saints Street, Hastings, East Sussex TN34 3BN (01424 465100); thecrownhastings.co.uk

The Globe Inn Marsh
Rye, East Sussex

On the edge of the medieval town of Rye lies a pub of tongue-in-cheek-cuteness: a clapboard-covered dream with nooks and log fires for winter and a beer garden for summer. The Globe Inn Marsh, refurbished in April of this year, may be quirky, it may also serve food – but it takes its beer seriously. In spite of not really having a bar.

Instead, here in this cornucopia of carefully-curated clutter you will find a handcrafted 'beer font' made of galvanised steel, with burnished copper tundishes, taps and pipes. Across the serving passage are the handpumps, with the barrels sitting on display. There's English Garden, from Franklins Brewery, hoppy but with undertones of biscuity malt, made in a microbrewery housed in a converted milking parlour in nearby Bexhill. Locally sourced is the theme here and so we have First in Last Out Gold (which goes by its acronym Filo) from Hastings just along the coast, a light bitter with hints of elderflower.

We had walked along the dunes at Camber Sands, eschewing Pontin's and its Bluecoats for a stomp up across the marsh and into this East Sussex town, one of the prettiest on the British coastline and a Cinque Port to boot. Not far from Landgate Arch, which you walk under to enter the town proper (for centuries Rye was an island, its only connection to the mainland through Landgate at high tide) we found the Globe Inn Marsh on Military Road, a street of red-bricked terrace houses that has been around since 1834. Inside, little punch cups were offered with tasting samples of the various different guest ales –

which frequently rotate. There was Hastings Handmade 22 Waimea pale ale, and Hooker's Hooch, a dark bitter brewed in Tonbridge. Kent ciders were heavily featured as well as English wines from local vineyards such as Chapel Down and Biddenden.

Rye once played an important role in the country's defences, but these days the warships have gone, the town's shoreline now the home to a fishing fleet. And the decor of the Globe reflects this – there's lobster pots as light shades, buoys hanging on the wall, Rye Fisheries window boxes and candelabras made from old wine bottles.

The Globe does have a big food offering, but from our visit there's still a good bit of work to do on both the cooking and the service (long waits for so-so food). But as a pub, it's a joy: a joy where they say tired dogs are welcome at their hearth. And it's not just a pub – you can pop in here and buy a pot of local jam. As they say in their bumpf: 'a pretty little pub on the edge of the marsh and not far from the sea'. But it is not just pretty, it's a cracking wee pub too, especially for tired old dogs like us.

Audrey Gillan, 8 November 2014

10 Military Road, Rye, East Sussex TN31 7NX (01797 225220); globeinnmarshrye.com

The Three Chimneys
Biddenden, Kent

Observant visitors may be puzzled by The Three Chimneys pub outside the village of Biddenden in the Weald of Kent. Only two chimney stacks top this ancient free house (circa 1420). A coded explanation is provided by the pub sign showing a French soldier looking at a three-armed signpost.

It refers to the Seven Years' War (1754–63), when the 3,000 French prisoners incarcerated in Sissinghurst Castle were allowed as far as the pub where three roads, or *trois chemins*, meet. Sceptics have doubted the likelihood of an enemy's phrase taking root but no better explanation has been found. However, as you duck under the low beams, you will find three fires – two log-burners and, in the pleasingly plain public bar, a mighty inglenook.

Adnams Best (3.7%), Adnams Oyster Stout (4.3%) and Biddenden cider (8.4%) are sold from casks behind the bar (there is no cellar but refrigerated probes produce a similar chill), along with a solitary guest ale, such as Good Health Bitter (3.8%) from Batley, West Yorkshire. Ordering a pint from the bar framed by swags of dried hops, the taller drinker is liable to be crowned by a Dionysian wreath.

'It's not what you do to a pub, it's what you don't do,' is the admirable view of the guv'nor Craig Smith, who packed in his City job to take over the pub in 1999. 'Adnams has been sold here for 40 years. There would be a riot if I took it out. We get through ten barrels a week so it's always fresh.' His conservatism extends to afternoon closing. 'I liked the old licensing hours. They gave a focal point.'

Though the beer is averagely priced (£3.15 for the splendid, ruby-red Best), you have to tread wary with the food unless you stick to crisps (90p) or soup (£4.95), which on the day of my visit was a sustaining red lentil broth accompanied by good butter and great wedges of Windmill loaf from Avards Bakery, Lamberhurst.

A casual caller whose eye is lured by local sausages (E.C. Wilkes of Cranbrook) with dauphinois potatoes and green beans will find himself shelling out £19.95. Welsh rarebit with poached pear salad costs £7.95, while rib-eye steak and trimmings is £20.95. The white wine list escalates from £19.75 to £57.75 for a Puligny-Montrachet. Oddly, there's nothing from the Biddenden Vineyard.

Voted Best Dining Pub in Kent four times in five years, The Three Chimneys draws a well-heeled clientele willing to pay the fairly hefty prices; with motors as high-powered as their chat ('Pierce Brosnan was on our beach'), they tend to head for the dining room, leaving the public bar for regulars and dogs. The landlord says he hopes to start selling sandwiches and bar snacks when the kitchen is extended later this year.

Christopher Hirst, 13 April 2013

Hareplain Road, Biddenden, Kent TN27 8LW (01580 291472); thethreechimneys.co.uk

Four Candles
Broadstairs, Kent

Tucked away on a residential street, a fair stomp from the Broadstairs seafront, sits the 'second smallest pub in Thanet'. Four Candles is just one tiny room in what was once a corner-site hardware store.

This is a micropub, and it is nigh on perfect, adhering to some simple rules – no lager, no bar, no jukebox – and the motto 'KisKis': Keep it small, keep it simple. Should a bit of banter not suffice as entertainment, there are board games to be toyed with, and a library offers books, both highbrow and bonkbuster, at 50p a go.

Even before you step across the threshold, you can see this place is just that wee bit different. There are two pitchfork handles painted above the lintel, along with the quote from an anonymous author: 'Beer is the drink of men who think, and feel no fear or fetter, who do not drink to senseless sink, but drink to feel better.'

And then there's the puntastic name, a homage to Ronnie Barker, who is said to have been inspired to write his famous sketch (in which a customer walks into a hardware store and asks for 'fork 'andles') by Broadstairs hardware store Harrington's, with its loose screws, tea-urn cleaning brushes and miscellaneous oddments of ironmongery.

Inside the tiny, sawdust-floored pub, the upturned metal bucket light-shades, and more crossed pitchfork handles, hammer the joke home. The walls are pinned with press cuttings on the micropub boom in Kent (which has flourished since a change in licensing laws a decade or so ago) and the windows are adorned with hundreds of beer mats.

The cask-conditioned ales are chalked up on a board – the line-up changes regularly. We try Goodness Gracious Me IPA from Herne's Goody Ales – hoppy, light in depth but bitter in length – which is described in the 'Our Customers Say' section of the blackboard as 'Your mouth goes boomboodiboom'. There's Spencer's Green Hop Gold and Maxim Double Maxim, all at £3 a pint – and all stored well in the adjoining room. Sparkling wine from Kent's Biddenden Vineyards is offered, along with their cider and apple juice.

We sit at high tables, swing our legs from the stools and pat ourselves on the back at discovering this gem. We eat the menu – Westgate pork pie and mustard (just £2), pork scratchings, Kent crisps and a plate of Ashmore cheeses from a nearby farmhouse producer – and raise a glass to the best the garden of England has to offer.

Four Candles was opened in 2012 by Mike Beaumont, but on our visit the warm welcome is offered by the lovely Janice, all dotty dress and pinny, who says, without us even asking a question: 'I'm really into ale, darling. Yeah. It's a great place to work. The ales are great.'

They are great. Four Candles is great. And so is Janice.

Audrey Gillan, 8 March 2014

1 Sowell Street, St Peter's, Broadstairs, Kent CT10 2AT;
thefourcandles.co.uk

The Swan on the Green
West Peckham, Kent

What makes the perfect pub? It should be an ancient structure, say 17th-century, with a plain interior and wooden floorboards. Perhaps some fresh green hops hanging over the bar. There would be great beer from a microbrewery in the back yard, plus good, reasonably priced food made from local ingredients, though locals who just want a pint would be well catered for.

Add a warm welcome from behind the bar. Needless to say, there would be no music or fruit machines. Even chips might be banished to spare patrons their particulate-laden miasma. As for location, would a village green, where cricket is played in summer, be satisfactory?

Ironically, the popularity of the Swan on the Green, which dates from 1685, tends to detract from its perfection. So many patrons were drawn on an autumnal Thursday lunchtime that there was only one space left in the car park and one free table inside (a large, well-scrubbed affair that my wife instantly coveted: 'I wonder what sort of wood it is?' she murmured dreamily). The American trio at a neighbouring table kept up a stream of impenetrable golfing chat as loud as it was mystifying ('There was only one birdie all day') but the quality of the Swan's drink and food provided a more than adequate distraction.

The pub has been making its own beer since current owner Gordon Milligan took over in 1999. Until the end of this month, the brews will be made with a variety of single green hops – hurry, hurry. My pint of First Gold 5% (a 3.6% ABV version was also available) was robust with a suggestion of black treacle. Even more surprising was the chocolate-tinged Goldings Mild, not in fact all that mild at 4% ABV. 'If we made it any weaker it would go off in the barrel,' explained the brewer Paul Haynes.

My first bite of boar burger with smoked bacon and emmental (£9.95) told me that I was on to a good thing. Raised on nearby Kent Field Farm, the boar was rich and succulent. 'You chose the most popular thing on the menu,' said head chef Adam Freeman. 'We've sold 60 in the last four days. One boar makes 600 burgers.' My wife's duck salad (£9.95), laden with generous pink slices of breast, was equally acclaimed: 'Tremendous.'

Both these choices from the 'Light Bites' section of the menu were deeply satisfying, but hearty appetites can tuck into boar steaks, venison and other local game for a few quid more. Desserts include Swan's Mess (£5.75), which looked far more appetising than it sounds. The food is, however, far from compulsory. Leigh Taylor, the bar manageress, said that on Friday and Sunday nights, the mix of drinkers and diners was 'around 50:50'. The Swan is so good that I would not have broadcast the fact if it were not my job.

Christopher Hirst, 23 November 2013

West Peckham, Maidstone, Kent ME18 5JW (01622 812271); swan-on-the-green.co.uk

The Bottle House Inn
Penshurst, Kent

In the lush outskirts of Penshurst, Kent, a village so impossibly picturesque that it must surely be a regular setting for Marple-esque murders, you come across an unofficial sign pointing to two pubs. To the left, The Spotted Dog; to the right, The Bottle House Inn. The former, recommended by both a local and CAMRA (Campaign for Real Ale), was going to be the subject of this column until my wife and I stepped into the long, murky bar, where every table was occupied by diners.

'You'll have to eat in the dining room,' snapped a barperson, nodding at an empty adjunct. Declining this Siberia, we asked to sit at the bar.

'What, and eat?' she gasped in astonishment. Settling for half a pint apiece, we peered at the blackboard menu. It did not exactly get the juices flowing: 'Chicken bits in Provençal sauce. Sea bream in olive oil dressing.' We were further discouraged when we overheard the barperson taking the orders from an adjoining table. 'There's no risotto. The chef dropped it on the floor. So that's two bream in oil?'

Reversing swiftly out of The Spotted Dog, we followed the signpost's other arm, to The Bottle House, where our greeting in the light, modernised bar was as warm as the Dog's had been frosty. Although the building dates from 1492, its name comes from 1935, when work on an extension unearthed a vast midden of discarded ancient glassware.

Though it is undeniably a dining pub – a hefty ploughman's served on a long, rectangular plate looked good value at £9.95, as did a plump cheeseburger and fries for £10.95 – there was no sign of surprise when we ordered a single starter of devilled whitebait to share (£5.25).

Accompanied by a half of Westerham Brewery's Spirit of Kent, a golden ale (4% ABV) flavoured with nine different types of Kent hops, and a half of Stowford Press cider (4.5%), the artfully arranged stack of paprika-tinged tiddlers made a perfectly acceptable snack lunch. 'People are always welcome for just a drink,' said Paul Hammond, manager of this independent free house, though he admitted, 'The main locals' night is Sunday when they've space to themselves.'

Weather permitting, the casual drinker can also sit at one of the twenty tables outside. These are 'very popular in summer and, oddly enough, in snow,' said the duty manager. On a May afternoon somewhere between those two extremes, just one visitor was to be found enjoying the fresh air. With his pint and his packet of Salty Dog crisps (90p), he looked entirely content.

Christopher Hirst, 22 June 2013

Coldharbour Road, Penshurst, Kent TN11 8ET (01892 870306); thebottlehouseinnpenshurst.co.uk

The Queen's Arms
Cowden Pound, Kent

People who run good pubs generally have a lot of respect for the old ways. But few take it to such extremes as 88-year-old Elsie Maynard, landlady of the Queen's Arms since 1973.* Ever since Elsie's father Henry took over the tenancy in 1913, the family has refused to go with the flow. Newfangled nonsense like lager, jukeboxes and flavoured crisps never crossed the threshold. But at a time when twelve pubs every week are closing, this time-warp has thrived.

Only one type of beer is sold on draught, Adnams Bitter, and there are never more than six optics. Cash goes into coffers and crisps are limited to salted only. Opening hours remain resolutely restricted and the pub only went decimal in the Nineties.

The brewery, Admiral Taverns, can do little about Elsie. They inquired about her plans a few years ago. 'I shall only be leaving here in a box,' she told them.

Elsie explained why the pub has thrived. 'The secret of running a successful pub is to be nice to the customers and listen to what they say,' she says. 'People love the pub because we know them all, we've known their fathers and their grandfathers.'

Elsie is keen to point out that the Queen's Arms hasn't been neglected, just loved and left intact. 'The public bar hasn't changed since the Thirties, the only difference is that we added toilets. You used to have to go outside and use an iron pot at the back.'

Her stance on one topic in particular will delight ale

buffs and horrify many others. 'I've never had lager here and never will,' Elsie says. 'In the first place it was too expensive and my customers couldn't afford it. Real beer is made with hops.'

Nor will her hostelry become a gastropub while she is around. 'Never, I like the old fashioned way. All we've ever done in the way of food is bread, cheese and pickles. I did the pickles myself. One year I did 200lbs, I started in the August and just kept going. It was a lot of jars, but I sold them all.'

The Queen's Arms has been frequented by several less desirable people down the years, most notably the 'acid bath murderer' John Haigh who dispatched at least six victims in the Forties. Local vet and pub historian John Hawkridge says: 'He would turn up in a smart sports car with his latest girlfriend. He travelled from Crawley and liked the pub because it was quiet and in a pretty part of the world.'

Hawkridge often works behind the bar and, like other volunteers, does not get paid. He is joined by Dave Wood, who looks after the cellar, and Tim Bates, the 'timber man', who keeps the fire going in winter.

The pub's future is uncertain, as Elsie acknowledges. 'I hope it is still a pub in a hundred years' time but I think the brewery will sell it,' she said.

Simon Holden, 19 January 2013

*Sadly, Elsie died in 2015, but the pub is going strong and is essentially unchanged.

Hartfield Road, Cowden Pound, Edenbridge, Kent TN8 5NP; open Mon, Tue 5–10.30pm; Wed, Thu 5–7.30pm; Fri 5–9pm; Sat 5–7.30pm (or 11pm if a music night; see elsiesband.com); Sun noon–3pm; whatpub.com/pubs/TTW/24/queens-arms-cowden-pound

Greater London

The Hope
Carshalton

H ow many people does it take to run a pub? The traditional answer is two: a husband and wife, working around the clock.

At The Hope in Carshalton, however, the answer is 38 because this is one of the tiny number of places in Britain run by the local community.

Step into the bar billiards room at the back of the pub and hanging on the walls are not the usual, grumpy signs asking you not to bang your car doors or start singing as you stagger outside. Instead, there is a rather skilfully drawn illustration of all the people who have come together to keep The Hope, as it were, alive.

You sense something is different the moment you walk through the door. Instead of being met by a world-weary couple asking if you want beer or lager, the two men behind the bar invite you to take your time and choose the kind of drink you want.

And selecting one isn't easy. A quick totting-up of beer pumps comes up with at least seventeen different types of drink, none of them household names.

There is Goddards' Ale of Wight (3.7% ABV), Windsor & Eton's citrusy Knight of the Garter (3.8%), Siren Undercurrent (hints of grapefruit and apricot), fruity Dark Star Revelation (5.7%) and super-dark Kissingate Six Crows (6.6%), not forgetting three ciders, two lagers and one perry. Oh, and eleven wines, seven rums, six whiskies and five gins.

There are two or three doors' worth of peanuts and

other snacks, and the food is half the price you might pay in a rural pub. Beef stew, chicken stew, liver, moussaka and shepherd's pie all come with a choice of potatoes plus salad, and a price tag of £6.50 to £7.50. Chilli con carne, chicken curry, sausage cassoulet and chicken chasseur squeeze under the £6 barrier.

Another appealing feature is that different groups sit in different areas. At lunchtime, turn left on entering and you are among the 50- to 70-year-old regulars who all have stories to tell about their starting wage (£4 a week in 1964) and complaints about how Alf Garnett isn't allowed on the telly any more.

If sentimental returns to the Sixties don't appeal, seek out the 20- to 40-somethings around the corner (there are a lot of corners) getting stuck into their boss, or the way their mother is driving them around the bend, over a fruity kriek or draught lager (they currently have Bavo pilsner from Belgium, and a German Helles beer, Hacker-Pschorr, from Munich – there is a 'beercam' on the website with updates).

So although The Hope isn't as large as some of today's mega-bars, everyone has an area they can call home. Of course, you could stay in your living room and have online conversations with people on the other side of the world.

But if you're interested in the people who live just down the road – your community, in other words – then a place like The Hope is just what you need.

Christopher Middleton, 5 December 2015

48 West Street, Carshalton, Surrey SM5 2PR (020 8240 1255); hopecarshalton.co.uk

The Jolly Woodman
Beckenham

The unspoilt pub that we search for in the country, usually in vain, may be found on your doorstep – at least if your doorstep happens to be in the depths of south-east London. According to one online appreciation, the Jolly Woodman has 'the feel of a rural pub', but it is tucked away on a side street in suburban Beckenham. When it opened in 1840, the stucco-clad ale house consisting of a single L-shaped room would have been in the Kentish countryside. Now, particularly at lunchtimes and weekday evenings, it is a near-miraculous survivor, a place of quiet sipping and chat.

What makes the Woodman so special is what it lacks: no music, no TV (aside from big sporting events), no carpet, no chips and no games machines. Less is more, though, as landlord Joe Duffy assured me, making a great pub doesn't merely mean chucking stuff out. 'We don't open on Mondays until 4pm so we can strip everything down and clean all the pipes.' Timothy Taylor Landlord and Harvey's Sussex Bitter are always on tap. Guest bitters at the time of my visit included Adnams Southwold and Kotchin from the Cronx microbrewery in Croydon. Online plaudits for the Woodman's beer testify to Duffy's skill as a cellarman.

With his grown-up children Katie, Michael and Maura behind the bar, service is prompt and friendly. Katie is responsible for the sole hot dish (£7.50) served at lunchtime – jerk chicken on the day of my visit was preceded by shin of beef, smoked haddock and mussels cooked in beer. Amply compensating for the lack of choice, the generous, tasty dishes are cooked from scratch with fresh ingredients every morning. Equally substantial sandwiches, ranging from ham or cheese (£2.75) to what Duffy terms the 'cholesterol special' of bacon, egg and black pudding (£3.75), are served throughout the day.

On a recent afternoon, a roaring coal stove ('Actually, it's gas,' Duffy admitted) warmed a sprinkling of customers on the benches and stools that surround the pub's well-scrubbed tables. A dartboard was available for 'arrows' fans. Shelves of paperbacks sold in support of the local hospice provided entertainment for solitary drinkers. 'You should be able to read a book or a newspaper in a pub,' said Duffy. 'Elderly ladies should feel comfortable here.' And they do.

It should, however, be admitted that 'unspoilt' does not mean 'undiscovered'. Duffy says the pub can seat 40 (perhaps a slightly generous estimate) but on Friday nights 'close to 100' will squeeze in. During the showing of Six Nations rugby matches (Duffy is a former player), the pub virtually comes apart at the seams with vocal polyglot contingents. Choose the right time, however, and you can find a corner of alcoholic heaven on a back street in Beckenham.

Christopher Hirst, 23 February 2013

9 Chancery Lane, Beckenham BR3 6NR (020 8663 1031); facebook.com/pages/The-Jolly-Woodman-Beckenham/177610388947754

The Ivy House
London SE15

Two years ago, this barn-sized neo-Georgian boozer was in a parlous state. Or rather, by all accounts, two years ago it was trundling along nicely. Then, in April 2012, its owners served a week's notice on the tenants and announced they were selling up to developers. With an easeful whisper of barathea on burnished leather, the local branch of CAMRA slid off their bar stools and got the pub Grade II-listed by English Heritage. This was quite justified on conservation grounds, the pub's Thirties interior being unusually intact (oak panelling, basalt fireplaces, stained glass, spittoons and all). It was also a brilliant stalling tactic, as tight rules on planning consent would surely impede the buyers in their dastardly scheme to gut the building and turn it into flats.

Meanwhile, a consortium of locals had the pub declared an Asset of Community Value under the Localism Act 2011. This bought a six-month grace period when the developers, outflanked by CAMRA's listing gambit, gave up and decided to sell the pub on. During this time the locals raised nearly a million quid, £180,000-odd of it out of their own pockets, bought the Ivy House themselves last March and opened it in the summer. It is run by a professional manager, but owned by the community: the first such set-up in London, and maybe the country. When the project received an English Heritage Angel Award (in a scheme supported by *The Telegraph*) before Christmas, it was obvious that here was a case of heritage having a use and a purpose, something interwoven with people's lives, something that matters in a more than purely aesthetic or curatorial sense.

So far, so virtuous. But – to quote, in its entirety, Kingsley Amis's catechism of literary merit – is it any good? On my first visit it all seemed a bit middle-class, with a bewildering array of craft beers and a CV appended to every bar snack. This might not matter except that (a) the neighbourhood is pretty diverse, with little Victorian terraced cottages along one side of Stuart Road, and some grittily monumental Seventies social housing on the other; and (b) the pub is enormous, and will have some hefty overheads – they will want it to be as full as it can be.

On a second visit I found a bigger and more varied crowd, tucking into their Pieminster pies and generating a warm fug of jollity on a cold night. The big back bar has a proper, blowsy, *Good Old Days*-ish stage. A poster on the wall records the legendary Dr Feelgood playing here in the Seventies, and forthcoming gigs include another pub rock giant, John Otway, as well as Los Pacaminos, fronted by the pride of Luton, Paul Young. It is still early doors for this noble enterprise, but if you're in south London, you could do a lot worse than lend it your support.

Keith Miller, 18 January 2014

40 Stuart Road, London SE15 3BE (020 7277 8233); ivyhousenunhead.com

The Three Stags
London SE1

Y ou know The Three Stags isn't your usual kind of pub the minute you step into the little glassed-in corner booth marked 'Chaplin Corner'. This is the snug bar where the great silent comedian's father, also called Charles, is said to have sat and drunk, in between engagements as a music-hall artiste.

Hanging on the wall is a black-and-white photograph of the film star his son went on to become, complete with bowler hat and little black moustache.

Also hanging on the wall is a framed text explaining that Chaplin Senior did not merely like a drink, but that he was a helpless alcoholic who died aged 37 from cirrhosis of the liver, when his son was just twelve.

This is not the kind of sugary testimonial that the tourists who come in here from the Imperial War Museum across the road may have been expecting. Nor are they likely to be prepared for the fact that, despite being built in Victorian times (1891), this high-windowed establishment has some very 21st-century eco-credentials.

Not only are the herbs and vegetables served in the pub grown within a two-mile radius of it; they are delivered by bicycle within an hour of having been plucked from the ground.

All the meat served is free-range; all the fish certified caught with rod and line rather than industrial-sized nets.

Bottles and cartons are recycled once used, all scraps are composted, and if you don't eat all your food, you're given a doggy-bag in which to take it home.

Oh, and there are beehives on the roof.

'Very popular, those hives,' says the landlord. 'We've had to add another two storeys to accommodate all the bees. Of course you know what their worst enemy is, don't you?' Pollution? Pesticides? Exhaust fumes? 'No,' he shakes his head darkly. 'Man.'

In keeping with the pub's personality, the food is clearly prepared with care; chips come served in attractive little blue mugs, while the chicken pieces inside my baguette (£8) are freshly barbecued, and The Three Stags is the proud holder of the Waterloo Quarter Food Festival Best Burger title.

There are plenty of international beers on tap (Leffe, Hoegaarden, San Miguel), but also a pair of lovely, if lesser-known, real ales. Deliciously honey-coloured Belhaven, brewed in Dunbar (3.2% ABV), and equally light, but slightly citrus-tasting St Edmund's bitter, from Greene King (4.2% ABV).

Not forgetting the home-grown house lemonade, which packs a powerful, if non-alcoholic punch, and could be served at the weekly music-for-small-children events which take place in the upstairs bar, on those days when there isn't a Pilates class or art exhibition. The décor here may be dark wood, but the atmosphere is all airy and light.

Christopher Middleton, 30 November 2013

67–69 Kennington Road, London SE1 7PZ (020 7928 5974); thethreestags.com

The White Swan
Twickenham

Love will be in short supply on the pitch this Valentine's Day when England front up to Italy in their first home fixture of the Six Nations. There will, however, be much backslapping bonhomie in the packed pubs of Twickenham during the build-up to the game.

The White Swan will be no exception. If previous match days are anything to go by, the road outside will be thronged with customers right across to the nearby bank of the Thames. From here it's a fair step to the stadium, but the diversion is worth the walk as long as you can drag yourself away well before kick-off.

What a pleasure it is to bask in all this elbow-bending room with the welcome warmth from an open fire. Also to gaze out of the window at a low, wintry sun spilling gold on the undulating surface of the river while savouring a pint of London Pride in a proper glass, as opposed to the plastic variety available on match days.

The only disappointment is the temporary absence of the Naked Ladies. 'Still settling,' says cellarman Steve Cunningham, not a man to be rushed when it comes to cask-conditioned ales.

For the said Ladies is a beer, made by local micro-brewery Twickenham Fine Ales and named after a group of marble statues frolicking around the fountain at nearby York House Gardens. They promise a 'good body and luscious aroma' according to the blurb on the pump-clip. We shall see.

The only Twickenham ale available this lunchtime is

Tusk, one of the new breed of keg IPAs, and a revelation to those of us weaned on the likes of Double Diamond and Red Barrel. Such is the sheer power of the hops that they overwhelm any lingering gassiness.

Tusk is not cheap, mind you. At £4.80 a pint, it's nearly a quid dearer than the Pride. Still, a half makes a satisfying digestif after my mixed pepper and smoked cheese frittata, served with chips and a mountain of red cabbage, from a menu that manages to be varied and imaginative without appearing too pretentious.

Solid wooden floors and log fires in both bars mark this out as very much a pub rather than a restaurant, despite the high celebrity count that you might expect in such a prosperous part of town. Keira Knightley has been spotted here. Johnny Depp and Keeley Hawes, too. Not together, mind you.

My only regret is that I've missed the bloke who comes in regularly with a live ferret peering out of his jacket pocket. This being 'Twickers' rather than Ambridge, I think we can assume that in other respects he bears no resemblance to Joe Grundy.

Chris Arnot, 7 February 2015

Riverside, Twickenham TW1 3DN (020 8744 2951); whiteswantwickenham.co.uk

The Finborough Arms
London SW10

The Finborough Arms prowls at the V-shaped junction of two busy London roads, its frontage reminiscent of a liner's prow stubbornly jutting out into the ocean of traffic that swirls about. It's of Victorian origin, built in 1868 when this part of Earl's Court was being developed.

Its interior, though, is very much of the now, with bare brick walls, a distressed wooden counter, gleaming beer founts, polished handpumps and a forest-green background of Fired Earth tiles glowering behind the bar.

However, as if to suggest that this on-trend décor shouldn't be taken too seriously, a variety of retro ads for long-gone breweries and, er, Bisto dot the walls. There is also one for that wizard of the water closet Thomas Crapper – he used to nip in for the odd bottle of bubbly in the 1890s.

While the ground floor of the Finborough is a comfortable space where good beer and wine are dispensed, the first is home to an acclaimed fringe theatre of the same name. Star-spotters out supping should take note: it's not unknown to see Dame Diana Rigg or Gyles Brandreth enjoying a sharpener before nipping upstairs.

On the evening I visit, however, there are no celebrities, just eager theatrical types and locals installed, limpet-like, at the bar while the landlord buzzes about greeting people and pouring beers. 'If Chelsea were playing at home tonight,' he tells me, 'we'd have an even more exotic mix of drinkers.'

There is something exhilarating about the diversity of

the pub's clientele. I share a few words with a young couple there for the night's play (something about censorship, I'm told) and am pleased to see they enjoy my beer recommendation: Hastings Stout, a rich and creamy, strong, dark beer with elements of liquorice and roast notes in the mix.

The juice of the barley is big here, and on my visit the cast of beers includes the aforementioned stout; Hobsons' peerless mild from Shropshire; the ultra-hoppy Lagunitas IPA from California; and the landlord's favourite lager, Tipopils, made near Lake Como by an Italian microbrewery. Meanwhile, the food is bar-snack nirvana: pork pies, chorizo-and-apple sausage rolls and scotched quail's eggs supplied by a local award-winning butcher. The pub also has a deal with next-door's pizzeria: wood-fired pizzas can be delivered for a discounted rate.

As I sip my second pint of Hastings stout, a bell rings. The theatregoers slip from the bar, their places taken by a new group of drinkers in search of liquid rather than cerebral refreshment. Up on the first floor, the actors are weaving their spell; but down here at the bar, as voices rise and fall, and glasses are drained, there is a different – but equally beguiling – form of magic in play.

Adrian Tierney-Jones, 24 January 2015

118 Finborough Road, London SW10 9ED (020 3417 0490); finborougharms.co.uk

CASK
London SW1

In a bid to keep expense to a minimum, I have selflessly chosen a pub this week that sits squarely on a ley-line running the two miles between the *Telegraph*'s offices and my flat. It probably doesn't require a Holmesian leap of logic to infer that this wasn't my first visit.

In fact CASK has been on my radar for some years – or rather, the structure it occupies has. It's one of a handful of postwar British buildings to be Grade II*-listed: part of Darbourne & Darke's Lillington Gardens Estate, where the revolutionary potential of reinforced concrete was tempered and made humane by the use of brick, and a wide variety of shapes and layouts, along with lashings of greenery, create an atmosphere very different from the dour, regimented quality of much Sixties social housing.

What is now CASK was the Pimlico Tram, a hefty, sculptural shape to get you round the corner from Tachbrook Street to Charlwood Street, with three high, chunky dormer windows giving on to a plain tongue-and-grooved interior.

Listing has meant that subsequent owners and licensees haven't been able to do much to the place. It's really just a room, painted a whiter shade of magnolia, with a bar at one end.

But there are bars and bars, of course – and the bar at CASK is a thing of astonishing, unrivalled plenitude, a very Xanadu for the beer lover: Beervana, if you will.

At this point I have to evince a degree of scepticism regarding the Craft Beer Conspiracy (CBC). Like the

British Cheese Conspiracy (BCC) of a few years back, it seems on first examination to be an entirely laudable thing, arising from nothing more sinister than a rebirth of regional pride and a desire for quality. But whereas the BCC saw a deluge of products into the marketplace that all looked different, yet all smelt and tasted more or less the same, with the CBC the issue is one of unfettered variety.

CASK has a 'beer menu' of preposterous, gigantic, *History of the English-Speaking Peoples* proportions. It sells beers from everywhere, tasting of everything. For this plenitude alone, it warrants inclusion in the Pint to Pint pantheon. Only – sometimes – it seems not to be that bothered about selling beer that tastes of beer. I have asked for 'a sort of clean, Pilsnery taste' there before, and received looks of incomprehension or outright pity. Having said that, the contemporary, Meantime London/Camden Hells style of lager, fresh and slightly hoppy, is usually well represented.

Food is hearty, blokeish and burger-centric – not cheap (£4 for a signature dish of 'chips with bacon dust'), but good. The clientele is strikingly various in age and gender. The staff are charming, courteous and enthusiastic, passing out advice and tasters, issuing little sage nods of approval or, in my case, tiny sibilations of dismay, as they move purposefully to and fro behind their thicket of handpumps.

Keith Miller, 28 September 2013

6 Charlwood Street, London SW1V 2EE (020 7630 7225); caskpubandkitchen.com

The Windsor Castle
London SW1

I t is boom-time for the 'handcrafted' products of breweries seemingly set up the day before yesterday. Yet there are still likely to be regulars in Yorkshire pubs proclaiming through froth-coated lips: 'I don't care what tha' says; there's nowt better than Sam's.'

Samuel Smith started brewing in Tadcaster in 1758 and, despite spawning what would become a much bigger neighbour, John Smith's, the company is going strong. It's still run by the Smith family; still brewing with water from the original well; still using wooden barrels; still opening pubs.

Those in London prove one thing for sure: there's nowt cheaper than Sam's. At the Windsor Castle, the Old Brewery Bitter is £2.90 a pint. Good head on it, too, and very malty in the aftertaste.

Tucked away behind Westminster Cathedral, the pub used to be known as The Cardinal. After the Tadcaster takeover some four years ago, the change came. 'They found a fire insurance document in the cellar dating to the mid-1800s, showing that it was originally called the Windsor Castle,' says manager Mark Brecknock.

Having reinstated the name, the building was then restored to its Victorian prime. From the moulded ceiling dangle lamps that look as though they've only recently been converted to electricity. Etched glass panelling abounds, dividing the downstairs into a series of snugs and lounges, one of which harbours a log fire.

Furniture is weighty and discreetly decorative – dark

wood chairs with high backs and scrolled arms look as though they might accommodate a conclave of cardinals. Dog-collars are not unknown in here after Sunday Mass, apparently. And the local congregation have evidently forgiven the brewery for the name change. Well, I can think of worse places to refresh the palate after cleansing the soul.

Those seeking the Guinness of old Ireland might be disappointed. Prices are kept low in Smith's pubs on the understanding that you can have any beer you like as long as it's Sam's. The same goes for lagers, ciders and stouts.

At £3.40 a pint, the Extra Stout is 50p more than the bitter but a damn sight cheaper than most Guinness in central London. Good clean taste, too, and dry yet creamy. It competes well with my formidable steak pie from a no-nonsense menu, give or take the occasional 'hand-pressed' burger. The pie comes with chips or mash, cabbage or French beans, and a jug of onion gravy that softens the pastry. The meat is tender and flavoursome, enriched by having been cooked in ale. You know full well which one.

Chris Arnot, 28 November 2015

23 Francis Street, London SW1P 1DN (020 7834 7260)

The Cow
London W2

G et out there, the editor said, and do an Irish pub for
St Patrick's Day. Given that across most of the planet
the phrase 'Irish pub' is more or less synonymous with the
word 'pub' I anticipated no problem.

A long walk down London's Kilburn High Road later, I
wasn't so sure. When I first came to London (with a fiver
in my pocket, and my old dancing bag), this long, seething
canyon of brick was thickly seeded with sturdy late-
Victorian saloons.

Sometimes the doors would swing open as you walked by;
you'd see light refracted through cut glass, hear excitable
voices, even the strains of a fiddle.

The big old boozers mostly still abide – but all changed,
changed utterly.

Kilburn has largely resisted gentrification, or the main
drag has; but you can't fight the tide for ever. The Earl
Derby has a vase full of arum lilies on a scrubbed oak table,
and 'vinyl only' DJs. The Black Lion, which has one of the
best Victorian pub interiors in London, serves tapas, and
doesn't do draught beer at all. Other places are now shabby
and melancholy: Country & Western duos keen plaintively,
satellite TVs and slot machines gibber. Others still have
given up the game and become chicken shacks, shisha bars,
a Central Asian Brasserie.

Farther south, I thought the Brazen Head might do.
Named for the venerable pub in Dublin, its Hibernian
credentials are at least impeccable. It stands next door to
the Lisson Gallery, with its whitewashed windows like a

ghostly strip club. It's a perfectly serviceable place, with a bar, chairs, windows, floor – all the usual accoutrements. But it doesn't quite meet the exacting demands of the rubric printed above this column.

Presently The Cow hove into view, a welcome sight indeed. It is, let us not mince words, considerably less horny-handed than the *echt* Irish boozers of NW6. Instead of a folk session or Glen Campbell tribute act, you get Boards of Canada on an MP3 player; the excitable voices are west London rather than west Britain. There's a reasonably catholic, but by no means bewilderingly or passive-aggressively comprehensive, range of beers; and many different whiskies, including some good Irish ones such as Bushmills Black Bush.

The food is hearty and excellent: seafood, steaks which practically eat themselves and a few more structured dishes (a dining room upstairs offers more of the latter).

The Cow is an aristocratic fantasy of peasant life, as it were, like Marie Antoinette's dairy: an artless-seeming but acutely thought-through bricolage of hand-painted signs, vintage posters, off-black woodwork, a linoleum floor of slaughterhouse red. You could do a sociology PhD on the Gents alone.

It offers a gentle rebuke to, and constitutes a refreshing change from, the sepulchral good taste of the standard-issue bourgeois London pub, all Farrow & Ball and portion control. And it is – abidingly and consistently – a happy place.

Keith Miller, 15 March 2014

89 Westbourne Park Road, London W2 5QH (020 7221 0021); thecowlondon.co.uk

The Spaniards Inn
London NW3

There aren't many pubs which can claim to be both literary landmarks and geographical obstacles, but The Spaniards Inn is an exception.

Not only has it featured in both Charles Dickens's *The Pickwick Papers* and Bram Stoker's *Dracula*, but for many a decade, the building has caused traffic between Hampstead and Highgate to go all single file.

In less heritage-conscious parts of the capital, the council would long ago have removed the pointy bit of pub that protrudes into the road, as well as demolishing the redundant toll house opposite. But this is hill-and-history-friendly Hampstead, where the idea of eradicating something old and inconvenient is as unthinkable as high-rises on the Heath.

Recently, locals have been made anxious by the announcement that the Spaniards (built 1585) was due for refurbishment, which in these parts is seen as the architectural equivalent of a lobotomy.

The good news, though, is that the work took just five days, and you'd hardly know the difference. Go up to the first-floor dining room, and the floor and ceiling still slope in reassuringly opposite directions.

On the ground floor, too, the walls are still wood-panelled, and the high-backed pub pews still invest the interior with the air of old-fashioned intrigue. Rather more 21st-century is the way in which there are 'Reserved' signs on most of the tables, and you have to wait for your food order to be taken by young men in black uniforms, pushing the establishment not just over the line that separates pub from gastropub, but over the even more significant gap between drop-in boozer and book-in-advance bistro.

Mind you, this is a place which is used to laying down the law. The gardens at the back can pack in 300 people on hot days, when it's not so much a matter of customer care as crowd control. And don't forget the dog-washing machine in the car park, for the sprucing-up of canines whose coats have become a little unkempt while on walkies.

Of course, this is known for being a part of the world where the humans are well-heeled and the four-pawed rather pampered. Which explains why beer is £4 a pint: tasty Adnams Lighthouse at 3.5% ABV, and dark, caramelly Urban Dusk, at 4.6%, brewed by Redemption London. And why the food is prettily presented, but pricey, too: £14 for a cheeseburger, and £5 for a Scotch egg, albeit hot and crunchy on the outside, and beautifully warm and yolky in the middle.

Cross the road, and you've got lord-of-the-manor views down over the capital. When you come for a drink here, you're not just on high ground, you're genuinely upmarket.

Christopher Middleton, 16 February 2013

Spaniards Road, London NW3 7JJ (020 8731 8406); thespaniardshampstead.co.uk

BrewDog Camden
London NW1

I s it a pub or is it a beer bar? Well, Camden's branch
of BrewDog sells beer, lots of it, ergo it must be a pub.
However, real-ale handpumps are conspicuous by their
absence – this is a centre of 'craft keg', the new wave of
boldly flavoured lagers, IPAs and stouts influenced by the
American brewing revolution. So that makes it a beer bar,
right?

Whatever it is, it's found itself a mighty good spot,
just minutes from Camden High Street. The large shiny
windows are partly embossed with the Miro-style logo of
brewery owners BrewDog. As this is London, where pubs
change their identities as often as mid-period David Bowie,
chances are it has possessed several faces – migrating from
backstreet boozer through gastropub and now … into
something else entirely.

Naturally, BrewDog's beers take centre stage among an
ever-changing cast. Eight tall canister-like fonts dispense
their liquids, including a winter porter, Hardcore IPA and
the 18% Tokyo (sold in thirds). There are also several
American beers on tap, including the superb Port Street
IPA, plus a large selection of rare bottles.

I go for BrewDog's Punk IPA, a pale ale pulsating
with tangy, bittersweet notes reminiscent of grapefruit.
Further exploration yields lemon, orange, a sour-sweet
undercurrent and a bracing bitterness. It's a glass of
sunlight in contrast to the sleet outside.

As befits a brewery aesthetic strong on style and
'edginess', the décor is stripped-down minimalism:

concrete floors and a collection of austere tubular furniture distinctly at odds with the sort of comfortable sofas usually found in an upmarket country inn.

The high ceiling and muted white walls give a *trompe l'oeil* sense of space while the board games jammed into alcoves at the end of the room provide a homely touch. There's also an upstairs room for quieter conversation.

This sort of post-industrial warehouse chic can all too often be shorthand for coldness, but BrewDog Camden is a hotspot of friendliness as warm as any traditional bar. Several young people stand engrossed with their mobiles or lifting their glasses to examine their beers with the seriousness of art experts scrutinising a Schnabel. The Yin to their Yang is provided by the traditional pub types embedded in the sofas or at the bar scanning the incredible beer list. It all makes for an easy-going atmosphere.

Sadly I've had lunch so cannot make space for anything off the menu developed by *MasterChef* winner and beer guru Tim Anderson. The curry-rubbed burger sorely tempts. However, I can always find room for another beer. Port Street IPA or Hardcore IPA?

Frankly, who cares if BrewDog is pub, bar or Buckingham Palace? Just sit back and enjoy the beer – the damn fine beer.

Adrian Tierney-Jones, 26 January 2013

---

113 Bayham Street, Camden Town, London NW1 0AG (020 7284 4626); brewdog.com/bars/uk/camden

The Pig and Butcher
London N1

Food in pubs: the jury's still out, isn't it? I suppose most of us would concede that it's a good thing. Yet, surely, every time a pub edges too far towards restauranthood, something precious and irreplaceable is lost. There has been a lot of talk about Rubicon-crossing recently: the publican's equivalent is telling people they can't sit in some invitingly empty quadrant of the premises because they're not proposing to eat.

The Pig and Butcher stays – just – on the right side of this divide (let's call it the Publicon). It is an archetypal gentrified north London boozer: large clear windows, an understated colour scheme (Name That Farrow & Ball Paint Swatch is as popular in these parts as shove ha'penny was a century ago). A frothy plaster frieze, and a solitary cast-iron Corinthian column, plonked in the corner like a giant hatstand, bear witness to once-exuberant decor. Mismatched wooden furniture is artlessly scattered around a large and open bar.

There's a more overtly restauranty bit, with the obligatory open kitchen, off to one side; but you can eat the full menu wherever you go; and one can partake freely of the juice of grape, grain, fruit, veg etc. in the restaurant.

Food and drink alike are nicely judged: traditional with a twist, or a bit of one. The wine of the month when I visited was Lebanese; the beer of the week Scottish (Odell's 90/-). The latter, it should be noted, was priced at an asset-stripping £5.25 a pint, though prices generally don't seem too steep for this part of town. A veritable Holy Roman

Empire of German bottled beers, and a wideish range of wines by the carafe, complete an amiably wide alcohol offering.

As far as food goes, both pigs and butchers are much in evidence; they're not exactly holding back on the cow front, either. The signature bar snack is a 'beef sausage roll' with horseradish. An hors d'oeuvre of very good, very soft black pudding came with pickled apple; an excellent steak, dry-aged until it was probably starting to wonder whether Popes really are getting younger, was blasted to beggary on the outside, bluish-pink and satiny smooth within. With the latter item came a knife of colossal size, as if the carnivores of Islington were expected to vanquish their dinner in single combat before eating it.

To be able to enjoy food this good in something that retains the expansive, informal and (very faintly) louche qualities of a pub is something to be celebrated. But it's a delicate balance: too much Farrow & Ball, too many menus on clipboards, too much attentiveness from the waiting staff, and you might as well just get thee to a restaurant qua restaurant and have done with it. The price of liberty is eternal vigilance.

Keith Miller, 6 April 2013

80 Liverpool Road, London N1 0QD (020 7226 8304); thepigandbutcher.co.uk

The Grapes
London E14

The Grapes offers an intriguing mixture of intimacy and expansiveness. To the fore is a small, exotically etched bay window encompassing a seat just big enough for a couple. Beyond is a narrow wooden floor flanked by a shabby-chic table or two. And to the rear is a small balcony offering the blissful prospect of sitting with a pint on a sunny autumnal lunchtime, overlooking the Thames at high tide as it surges around the ankles of an Antony Gormley statue and slaps powerfully against the weathered London brick.

When the tide goes out, there's a pebbly beach from which Sir Walter Raleigh set sail on his third voyage to the New World. There has been a pub on the site since 1583, but the current building dates from around 1720.

It's part of a handsome terrace of Georgian Blitz survivors, among them the home of Sir Ian McKellen, co-owner of the Grapes with the director Sean Mathias (his former partner) and newspaper magnate Evgeny Lebedev. It was Lebedev who set up a meeting here between David Cameron and Stephen Fry to discuss gay rights in Russia shortly before the Winter Olympics. They dined in the restaurant upstairs where main courses are around 10 quid more expensive than those on the bar menu.

Downstairs, you can savour sausage and mash with onion gravy and 'pie of the day with chunky chips' for £7.50. The most popular dish, however, is fish and chips with mushy peas (£9.95) – Billingsgate haddock coated in a crispy batter whisked up from a recipe of venerable vintage.

And to wash it down? Five handpumps grace the central bar, two of which dispense guest beers. The regulars are Marston's Pedigree, Adnams Bitter and Black Sheep, the latter pulled without the tight, creamy head demanded by aficionados in Yorkshire. Still tastes pretty good to me.

On a shelf behind the bar is a stuffed fluffy cat, presented to McKellen by fellow thespian Patrick Stewart. The floor between the bar and the balcony is covered with red lino, the walls with pictures of Dickens and bookcases in which his works feature prominently.

The Grapes is described thus in the magisterial opening chapter of *Our Mutual Friend*: 'A tavern of dropsical appearance ... long settled down into a state of hale infirmity. It had outlasted many a sprucer public house, indeed the whole house impended over the water but seemed to have got into a condition of a faint-hearted diver who has paused so long on the brink that he will never go in at all.'

It's a century and a half since those words were quilled, but the dropsical tavern is looking remarkably hale – with no shortage of ale.

Chris Arnot, 4 October 2014

76 Narrow Street, London E14 8BP (020 7987 4396); thegrapes.co.uk

East of England

The Crooked Billet
Leigh-on-Sea, Essex

They look like lopsided jugglers, with a pint in one hand and a polystyrene cup in the other: one vessel full of the amber nectar, the other brimming over with bouncy little cockles dribbled with vinegar. Squinting in the early spring sunlight, they bear their precious cargo forward, scanning the rows of wooden tables for a spot to sit and feast.

For it is mostly beer and cockles that lead people to the Crooked Billet, in the Old Leigh quarter of the Thames Estuary town of Leigh-on-Sea – a fine pairing that, some say, rivals champagne and oysters.

Just a 40-minute train ride out into Essex from London's Fenchurch Street station brings you to this tableau of wharves, fishing boats, cockle sheds and mud flats: where the smell of marsh and ozone mixes with the waft from the smokehouses.

Step under the low-beamed ceiling of the Crooked Billet (the only pub in town not named after a fishing vessel) and you will find pumps offering a fine array of ales. A Nicholson's pub, its six handpumps offer Nicholson's Pale Ale, Adnams Southwold, Sharp's Doom Bar and regular guest ales, which can include Ha'penny's London Stone, or Rudgate Ruby Mild.

Should the sun not be shining, you can hog the fire and perhaps earwig on a salty old sea-dog giving his wisdom to one of the town's youths ('When I was your age I was living my life, making it full and joyous, not messing it all up like you'). Or sit and watch the tide turn from the bay windows that look out across the estuary.

Though I love the richness within, it is the terraces and seawalls outside that take me to the Crooked Billet time and again. Find a place to settle and send a pal to the Osborne Bros cockle stall and café, once a former stable mews which housed horses and carriages bringing casks of ale to the pub across the street.

For £5, I buy a half a pint of shell-on prawns, a polystyrene cup overflowing with cockles, four smoked sprats and a rollmop herring, and settle beside a wooden table with my pint. I eat and drink and watch as the sun dances on the thick brown silt beyond. The boats and bawleys lying beached at high tide on the sandbanks bring thoughts of the six similar cockling boats which, in the Forties, joined the 'little ships' of Dunkirk, each rescuing thousands of troops during Operation Dynamo.

Stories of old Leigh echo not just in the photos that line the walls inside this 16th-century tavern. You can hear them all around you. As the sun retreats, I return to the warmth of the fire and the mellow tones of the wise old sea-dog. Time and tide may wait for no man, but here in the Crooked Billet it seems to have stopped still, the better to attend to his stories.

Audrey Gillan, 2 March 2013

51 High Street, Leigh-on-Sea, Essex SS9 2EP (01702 480289); nicholsonspubs.co.uk/thecrookedbilletleighonsea

The Old Lifeboat House
Clacton, Essex

There are three things you need to know about the Old Lifeboat House, in Clacton. The first is that it's near the briny. Just a small triangle of municipal flower-bed-cum-traffic-island separates it from the North Sea. The second is that, in terms of décor, it is utterly frill-free. Behind an interestingly spired and portholed exterior lies a bare, rectangular room with brown chairs, brown carpet and severely double-glazed windows.

The third thing – and this is the one that makes this place shine out like a lighthouse on a foggy day – is that it changes its real ale selection almost with each tide. Testimony to this is to be found all over the walls. Whereas other seaside establishments might hang paintings of sailing ships and fishing boats, the Old Lifeboat House just sticks up beer mats. In the same way as people used to sew badges on their windcheaters, showing where they'd been, this pub puts up little cardboard mementoes of every draught ale that's been drunk here.

You can fill a pleasant half-hour just wandering around, reading the names. There's Salopian Treasure Trove, Penpont Silent Night and Daleside Square Rigger. Not to mention jokier ones, such as Hewitt's Urbane Gorilla, Woodforde's Once Bittern and Wolf Brewery's Granny Wouldn't Like It.

'I seem to like any beer from Cornwall, so I always have one Cornish ale on the go,' muses the landlord, and today it's Proper Job (4.5% ABV, from St Austell). This is a flavoursome IPA which, for me, takes the bronze medal, behind smooth, gentle Pendle Witch (5.1%, from Moorhouse's of Burnley) and alluring, fruity Abbot Ale (5%, from Greene King of Bury St Edmunds).

They don't just serve the beers, either: they promote them in a variety of mini-festivals; there are Real Ale and Strong Ale events, plus darts nights (two boards), live music evenings and a special, every-Wednesday offer of a pint for £2.60 instead of £3.10.

Despite the array of attractions to outsiders, a friendly community feel still pervades. Conversations among the handful of lunchtime drinkers revolve around what's on the television news, the relative comfort of clogs versus sandals, and one of the regulars' scheduled operation date.

Just a couple of hundred yards down the road are the delights of Clacton's fruit-machine pavilions (Gameshow, Magic City, the Gaiety Arcade). Not forgetting Tubby Isaacs' Quality Seafood Stall, plus a pier complete with big dipper, tenpin bowling alley and Gipsy Rosalee, the fortune teller. And not forgetting Armstrong's restaurant, dramatically suspended over the sea and offering a view of 48 rotating wind turbines on the horizon.

No shortage of noise and action, then, if you want it. Inside the Old Lifeboat House, though, it's an altogether quieter kind of seaside.

Christopher Middleton, 26 April 2014

39 Marine Parade E, Clacton-on-Sea, Essex CO15 6AD (01255 476799)

The Swan
Stratford St Mary, Suffolk

I've always treasured the tale of John Major and Boris Yeltsin turning up at a pub close to Chequers eager for a pint. It had shut for the afternoon and when Yeltsin's advisers banged on the door saying that the president of Russia was outside eager for a drink, the sceptical landlord within declared that he was the kaiser.

Back in 1736, I wonder if the Swan's boss was equally bolshie when George II dropped by in the middle of the night en route to London? Whatever words were exchanged, the king was let in and enjoyed a plateful of local sausages.

The road George came along was the old coach road that once darted through Stratford St Mary and straight past the Swan, which must have been great for passing trade, royal or not. Nowadays, the conveyor belt of the A12 takes traffic past this pretty village, in which the pub has been a focal centre since at least the 16th century.

The Swan certainly looks the part: the frontage is classic black-and-white half-timbering, while across the road the River Stour runs, willow trees aslant on quiet waters. It's not unknown for passing kayakers to drop in for a pint.

The low-ceiling, beamed interior of the main 'Drovers' bar is a comfortable and cosy space, and on the late Friday afternoon I visit there's a sine wave of conversation as a handful of drinkers review the week's events (there is another bar next door, and a dining room at the back of the pub). Suddenly one of the voices leaps like a flame from a struck match and the pub's book club is convened:

'It's sunny, the library has a terrace and the librarian has some new books. Thank Adnams it's Friday!' And off a trio of drinkers go.

The mention of Adnams means it's time for a beer. There are three cask ales: I ask for the Southwold brewery's Mosaic, a gleaming golden-copper colour, with plenty of tropical fruit on the palate alongside a Sahara-like dryness and bold bitter finish. The pub also serves Belgian, American and German beers alongside a selection of 120 wines, many of which are biodynamic.

The beer rouses my appetite. Will it be the creamy asparagus tart or the Cromer crab salad? Eventually, I go carnivore and choose the duck and puy lentils, a meaty, earthy ensemble which Ed the barman recommends I eat with a bottle of Rodenbach, a vinous, sweet-sour West Flemish red ale. The match is perfect (like the pub).

Meanwhile those on the A12 rushing on by to Colchester or Ipswich are missing a true gem. If you want locally sourced and seasonally influenced food in the company of artisanal wines and craft beers from both home and away (plus a book club) then I would follow George II's example. But go a bit earlier.

Adrian Tierney-Jones, 24 May 2014

Lower Street, Stratford St Mary, Suffolk CO7 6JR (01206 321244); stratfordswan.com

The Anchor Inn
Woodbridge, Suffolk

S trangely, the Anchor Inn in Woodbridge is not a seaside pub. Woodbridge is a riverside market town not quite on the Suffolk coast but on a tidal estuary. It does, however, have a harbour and quays and lots of boats, so its nautical connections are very evident. The Anchor also has a massive anchor pub sign on the brightly painted exterior.

As you enter the bar, which is right opposite Ferry Quay, you could be forgiven for thinking that the Anchor is quite a small pub, most likely suited to thirsty rather than thirsty and hungry customers. Down a few steps, however, at the side of the bar there is a smuggler's warren of rooms given over to restaurant tables.

The building dates back to the 18th century and has an old-world charm with dark wood furniture, flagstone floors and roaring fires. Standing or propped around the bar are a cast of regulars talking about renovating boats, scraping bottoms and other seafaring pastimes.

One of them is Gordon, a craggy mountain of a man with laughter lines on his face that you could drop anchor in. He runs a marine engineering business on the quay, although he seems to be able to turn his huge hands to almost anything, including repairs to the still-working 800-year-old tide mill.

Gordon bemoans the lack of dredging of the River Deben, which he blames on environmentalists. The harbour, he says, has been dredged for hundreds of years, but now that the practice has been curtailed in order to protect wildlife, the haven is silting up.

It is a lively discussion, fuelled by the Greene King cask ales on offer, including Abbot Ale and St Edmunds.

I choose a pint of IPA, which is hoppy with a fresh bitter finish. When I ask how his pint is, Gordon tells me that he came to bury St Edmunds not to praise it — and he takes a large gulp of the golden ale.

The menu is a mixture of English staples such as slow roast pork belly and Gressingham duck breast, and more exotic offerings such as Istana lamb curry with basmati rice, or seared wood pigeon. I choose a half-pint of locally smoked shell-on prawns, followed by local cod fillet with bacon and broad bean risotto.

All of these are simply excellent and enjoyed in the lively atmosphere created by a mixture of young and old people, many of whom are talking about messing about in boats and laughing about minor misfortunes on the water.

After a day of being a tourist, visiting the Riverside Theatre and the nearby Sutton Hoo Saxon royal burial ship, a walk along the riverside followed by a visit to The Anchor and a chat with the locals is a perfect way to spend the evening.

Ed Jowsey, 2 May 2015

19 Quay Street, Woodbridge, Suffolk IP12 1BX (01394 382649); theanchorwoodbridge.co.uk

The Village Inn
West Runton, Norfolk

If you'd gone for a pint at The Village Inn, West Runton in the Seventies or Eighties, you might have rubbed elbows at the bar with some wide-eyed young hobbledehoy en route to catch Black Sabbath or the Sex Pistols. A blue plaque on the pub commemorates the notorious West Runton Pavilion which once stood behind it, now demolished. If accounts of the Pistols' performance there are correct, though, I'd wager your trip to West Runton today will be more enjoyable, if less weighed down with pop-cultural significance.

In good weather the pub's enormous garden is a relaxing place to enjoy the sunshine, with enough space that it doesn't feel crowded even when full. The only drawback seems to be that on my visit, not all the pub's parasols were up. So put on sun cream and wear a hat – or, like me, you'll end up engaged in a game of non-musical chairs as you change tables every five minutes trying to find the best spot to avoid the sun.

Fortunately the pub is as roomy as the garden and it's no hardship to be inside even on a warm day. The front of the bar is adorned with the same flint that covers the outside of the building. Well-worn parquet floor makes the place feel lived-in and loved rather than tatty. We bagsy the curved window seat with faded brocade cushions and frosted glass which cleverly avoids the goldfish bowl effect. A few pints of Grain Brewery's hoppy session beer Oak (3.8%) provide perfectly served hydration (there's no sloppy beer dripping down the outside of the glass here) but there are also three or four other beers to choose from including other Norfolk offerings from the likes of Woodforde's and Lacons – both good breweries making a range of fine ales.

Being right on the north Norfolk coast, between the seaside summer holiday hotspots of Sheringham and Cromer, The Village Inn does an extraordinarily good job of getting the balance between locals and visitors right, although you can easily spot the regulars clustered on stools chatting to staff from the end of the bar. Doubtless they also make the most of the pub's food which can be partaken of in garden, restaurant or bar.

The menu isn't cheap, but you get what you pay for: my mariner's pie at £12 felt worth the money, and my husband declared himself satisfied with his scampi and chips. Other options are Cromer crab dishes from £7 and Sunday roasts from £11.50 (best book for these as they regularly sell out).

While waiting for our food we pass the time with the pub's endearingly battered board games, substituting a bottle cap for a missing rook so we can play chess. When I was a child a trip to the pub with my parents often seemed like a day out in itself: food, drink, games to play and the run of a huge garden. The Village Inn perfectly captures that feeling. Be sure to allow yourself enough time to enjoy it.

Sophie Atherton, 25 July 2015

West Runton, Cromer, Norfolk NR27 9QP (01263 838000);
villageinnwestrunton.co.uk

The Lifeboat Inn
Thornham, Norfolk

Early evening at the Lifeboat and long-standing regular David Thompson has taken delivery of what looks like an enormous mug of tea. The mug is opaque, as indeed is the murky liquid inside it, which turns out to be draught cider. David tops it up every now and then with a clear, transparent substance from a bottle that he keeps close at hand. 'Lemonade,' he assures me.

His first visit to the Lifeboat in Thornham was in 1943, when he was four years old. 'It's only been a pub since the Twenties,' he confides with the air of one who likes to puncture the illusions of visiting holidaymakers. 'It was a farm before then.' Several centuries before then, judging by the gnarled state of the low beams and the even lower doorways.

Tankards – pewter and brass – dangle from the beams in the intimate front bar. Implements, nautical as well as agricultural, are more in evidence under the sloping ceiling of the room beyond. But despite the pub's name and the pictures of boats being rescued from choppy seas on the wall of the candlelit snug, no lifeboat crew was housed here in living memory. 'The nearest one is four miles up the road in Hunstanton,' David confirms.

Certainly the edge of the North Sea is a hell of a walk away, albeit through one of the most distinctive landscapes in all England. How pleasant it is to sit outside the Lifeboat knowing that salt marshes and sand dunes lie just beyond the car park – to be explored, perhaps, once I've seen off this pint of Woodforde's Wherry bitter, a perfect blend of malt and hops that quenches the thirst while building the appetite.

Maybe we'll do that walk a little later, now that I've finally been joined by my wife who is reading out tempting extracts from the menu. My slow-cooked pork belly with seared king scallops goes extremely well with the 'green apple purée'. The crackling is so more-ishly crispy that it poses a greater threat to the heart than the back fillings. She, meanwhile, has filleted the sea bass draped across her plate and is savouring its flavour with some relish.

Somehow she still has room for a chocolate brownie with vanilla ice cream which I feel obliged to help out with. Goes extremely well with Greene King's Abbot, one of those heavy, brooding beers with a slightly sweet undercurrent.

We appear to be one of the few couples here without a dog. Labradors, pugs and setters are sprawled across the tiles in the canine Land of Nod, exhausted perhaps by that walk from the Lifeboat to the sea.

Chris Arnot, 27 June 2015

Ship Lane, Thornham, Norfolk PE36 6LT (01485 512236); lifeboatinnthornham.com

The Railway Arms
Downham Market, Norfolk

Most pubs have a fairly fixed clientele. The Railway Arms, however, does not. The clue lies in the name. It's barely ten feet from the pub door to the London-bound train. By its very nature, this is a venue where people are on the move.

This transience, however, brings benefits. Instead of providing a home for stolidly silent pint-nursers, the Railway Arms inspires an altogether chattier class of customer.

On the day of my visit, the little bar was packed with a party of eleven Masons on their way to the capital. Clad in identical black suits and toting identical black suitcases, they fortified themselves for the journey with bacon rolls.

Meanwhile, the young barman Callum (this is a family-run place) was scurrying back and forth through the arch-way that separates pub from café. You want a cup of coffee or a KitKat, and he can serve you straight away. For a glass of cider, though, he has to make his way to the tap room.

Here, a wall of different cider and perry kegs await the call. None of the beers on sale is what you'd call a household name. (Go into your local and ask for a half of delicious Hogan's Poachers Perry, 5.8% ABV, or Tumbledown Dry, 5.2% ABV, or Gwynty Ddraig – it means two trees in Welsh – and you'll get uncomprehending looks plus the reply 'We've got Strongbow'.) All cost a keen £3.40 a pint.

The reason for this recondite cider offering is that the Railway Arms is the 2013 CAMRA cider-and-perry pub of the year. It's small and cosy (a dozen people is a crowd), and as well as offering six types of apple-and-pear-themed alcohol, it has an overspill library room, where you can sit, read books and magazines, and miss any number of trains.

That said, there's no danger of not reaching your destination, given the unusual opening times. The flow of cider only happens in the mornings (10am till just after midday) and from 3.30pm–5.30pm in the afternoons. The only evening the pub shows the green light for drinkers is Saturday (6pm–10.30pm).

Maybe it's the limited drinking time, maybe it's due to the passing-stranger atmosphere, but the pub is as convivial and chatty as your front parlour. Within five minutes, I was talking tattoos with one of the regulars, as he demonstrated the entire cast of *The Simpsons* inked on one leg, with numerous Sixties cartoon characters on other limbs.

Next to arrive was a woman who pronounced herself familiar with the tattoos, and wanted a coffee before getting on the London train (she goes every Tuesday). Unlike most pubs, the drink here seemed to gently oil, rather than rocket-fuel, the conversation. Mind you, it was only 11.30 in the morning.

Christopher Middleton, 30 May 2015

Downham Market Station, Railway Road, Downham Market, Norfolk PE38 9EN (01366 386636); railway-arms.co.uk

The Brewery Tap
Peterborough

It's not every day that you find yourself savouring Thai food with English draught beer in a former labour exchange.

From the outside the building is austere Thirties in solid red brick. No nonsense. Apart, that is, from a huge and lurid banner advertising Green Devil IPA (6% ABV), draped around a hop silo towering over the roof.

Welcome to The Brewery Tap, Peterborough. Which is a bit baffling, as the brewery in question is Oakham. Relocation from Rutland to Cambridgeshire came about in 1998, by which time it had outgrown its origins in the biggest town in England's smallest county. (One of the partners, meanwhile, had married a Thai restaurateur from London and more chefs were lured from her homeland. Hence the preponderance of spicy food in what might be called Oakham's Thai-ed houses.)

Growing demand for its beers is hardly surprising if their showing here is anything to go by. JHB, or Jeffrey Hudson Bitter (3.8%), is light in colour yet full of flavour with a dry and citrusy finish.

Not quite as citrusy as the slightly stronger Citra (4.2%), but then the clue's in the name. CAMRA's Champion (gold) Beer of Britain, 2014, more than holds its own against the spices of the crispy duck salad, cooling lip and tongue in the process.

My determination to go easy on the food to leave room for the beer has been somewhat undermined by an amiable couple from Spalding who've been ploughing through a

veritable Thai banquet. 'Have our potato wedges,' says he.
'We couldn't eat another thing,' says she, handing over the
remains of the chilli dip as well.

Ah, well. Glad to help.

There's just room for a half of Bishop's Farewell, a
judiciously balanced and full-bodied 4.6%, and just time
for a browse around.

The internal décor is as different from the building's
exterior as the current clientele from the flat-capped and
mufflered jobseekers of the Thirties. A floor of light wood
and polished stone is bordered by startling black and white
tiles and topped here and there by comfortable leather
sofas.

There are settles around the outside walls and the
function room is separated from the main bar by two
handsome carved doors worthy of the nearby cathedral.
Bought on eBay, apparently, as indeed was the even more
ornate wooden panel hiding the gas and electricity meters.

But the *pièce de résistance* is the glass wall separating the
bar from a micro-brewing plant. You may just catch them
producing a short run of seasonal ales in there. Or, like
me, you can simply speculate how much elbow grease went
into keeping those sizeable, silvery vats so shiny before
regretfully bending my own elbow to see off the last of the
Bishop's Farewell.

Chris Arnot, 19 September 2015

---

80 Westgate, Peterborough PE1 2AA (01733 358500);
www.thebrewery-tap.com

East Midlands

The Soar Bridge Inn
Barrow upon Soar, Leicestershire

Early on a Friday night and the Soar Bridge Inn is
warm, cosy, packed and buzzing with conversation.
There's no 'in' crowd here – everybody is 'in': young,
middle-aged and veterans alike. The bar, brightly lit and
beautifully set out, beckons, straight ahead. There's a
glowing log fire and I can see a few dogs dozing under
chairs. I've never set foot in the place before, but one or
two people nod and smile a welcome. I know already this is
going to be a good night.

Everards is a regional, long-established family brewery,
known for its enthusiasm for its cask beers, even through
the bleak keg years. It has more than 170 pubs and the
Bridge is one of them. There's a fine selection of half a
dozen of Everards beers here, each sentried by its own
pump and colourful clip. I'm spoilt for choice, so I go for
something light, Sunchaser, a golden vision at 4%, which
turns out to be a fine aperitif. 'We sell that to the lager
drinkers,' says the young man behind the bar, 'to try and
convert them to real beer.'

The pub majors on hearty, inexpensive comfort food.
Friday night is Fish and Chip Night, and a whole long
corridor of folk are grazing contentedly. There's also
Steak Night, Curry Night, Home Made Pies Night and on
Sundays, well, traditional roast – what else?

I'm here for the beer, though, of course; but there's
something else.

'Life isn't all beer and skittles,' wrote Thomas Hughes in
his excruciating novel, *Tom Brown's Schooldays*, circa 1857,

'but beer and skittles, or something better of the same sort, must form a good part of every Englishman's education.'

Personally, I've never understood that bit about 'something better of the same sort'. There isn't anything much better.

The Bridge is an enthusiastic skittles pub – there are different teams playing here four nights a week through the winter. This is Leicestershire's very own game, Long Alley, with nine pins and a barrel-shaped cheese, which the players insist on calling a ball. Funny ball. It is very difficult to control and bounces off in all sorts of odd directions, but some of the players tonight, in the Soar Bridge 'A' team and Syston Conservative Club 'B', are magicians. This is a league match, serious stuff.

One or two players note my pale and interesting drink and suggest I should go on to Everards' Tiger Bitter (4.2%). It's tastier and more robust, they say. I do, and they are right. Presently, I am advised to try Original, which is even more robust and interesting, at 5.2%. Goodness me, three pints – I've been binge-drinking again.

Arthur Taylor, 8 February 2014

29 Bridge Street, Barrow upon Soar, Leicestershire LE12 8PN (01509 412686); everards.co.uk/our-pubs/the-soar-bridge-inn-barrow-on-soar

The Exeter Arms
Derby

The Exeter Arms is a survivor. This was once a bustling area, but now only the Exeter Arms and a Thirties block of 'heritage' flats remain amid the modern sprawl of car parks and offices. On first impression, you could say it cuts a lonely figure.

However, it's certainly not friendless.

It's one of the most popular ale pubs in Derby, winner of copious awards.

As I step through the door, I'm immediately warmed by the welcoming ambience of a traditional pub: the flooring is red tile in places, black-and-white chequered in others; seating is comfortable wooden settles and banquettes, and a variety of drinking spaces are arranged off the bar.

I presume they were once various snugs and bars before being opened up – but they still retain a cosy and comfortable feel. The place has been brought up to date gently, sensitively.

There are six cask beers – just the right amount to satisfy the most David Livingstone-like of beer explorers while retaining superb quality. The local brewery Dancing Duck owns the pub, and its beers take pride of place at the bar, joined by Marston's Pedigree (brewed down the road in Burton) and Thornbridge's Chiron.

There is robust pub food at its best. We're talking ham, egg and chips, or shepherd's pie with spicy parsnip mash. However, I plump for the British tapas board – it sounds gastro-ish but comprises a suitably down-to-earth Scotch egg, home-made sausage roll, pork pie and Stilton, all locally sourced.

I also order a glass of DCUK, a sprightly, fruity pale ale brewed by Dancing Duck. 'It's like grown-up fruit juice,' says one of the regulars at the bar. I look around the open bar, noting old prints of Derby, a ceramic duck and – curiously, in this urban setting – a set of antlers, and he whispers to me: 'Have you seen next door?'

I follow him into the beer garden at the back and through to another drinking space. I'm in the front parlour of what was once the cottage next door, formerly the home of a local family. There's a fireplace, prints on the wall, bric-a-brac, bare brick and a sense of calm. It feels as if it is just waiting for the family to pop in again.

Adrian Tierney-Jones, 8 June 2013

Exeter Place, Derby DE1 2EU (01332 605323); exeterarms.co.uk

The Pattenmakers Arms
Duffield, Derbyshire

O ne minute, manageress Emily Bowler is rushing to
find a high stool for a village elder who is making slow
but steady progress from the front door to the bar; the next
she's off down the cellar steps to re-emerge with a three-
pint jug of Bass for myself and two old pals I've bumped
into on the train from Derby.

Bass straight from the barrel: now there's a tipple to
savour for connoisseurs of what was once the best-known
beer in the world. Alas, Bass has been allowed to wither
on the hop-pole in recent decades: it's now brewed under
licence by its one-time rival, Marston's. Very acceptably,
it must be said, on its showing at the Pattenmakers Arms,
where it's available by jug or pump.

There are at least seven other handpumps. One dispenses
Marston's Pedigree; the rest are guests. Among them today is
Big Cat from Byatt's of Coventry, a well-balanced pale bronze
bitter, which has just been recommended by Mick Lesley, one
of a rum bunch of regulars ranged around the horseshoe bar.

Mick worked for Bass for 30 years and ran many a
tied house for them. 'But this is the best pub I've been
in,' he tells me as we stroll out to inspect the somewhat
rudimentary skittle alley at the top of the car park.

The building we're standing behind was built in the early
20th century, when horses were still more common than
cars and effluence was more evident than affluence on the
streets of this and many a village. Hence the need for a
'patten', a metal frame clipped on to the sole of the shoe to
raise it above the filth.

No need for pattens today. The carpet that dominates the Pattenmakers' floor space remains comparatively unsullied. There's a small tiled area at one side of the bar and a parquet floor in a smokeless former 'smoke room' with etched and stained windows.

Licensee Claire Muldoon has greatly increased trade since taking over in 2008 by offering not only fine beers and a warm welcome, but homely lunchtime meals at prices you'd pay for bottled water in some London restaurants.

Her reward? A 42% rent increase. Enterprise Inns has since backed down in the face of a huge petition and the intervention of the local MP, Pauline Latham, who raised the issue with Business Secretary Vince Cable.

Claire is away on a well-deserved holiday today, but Emily is covering admirably. One minute she's ferrying from the kitchen some very fine faggots in a rich gravy; the next she's off down the cellar again to top up our jug.

Good job we're on the train.

Chris Arnot, 13 September 2014

Crown Street, Duffield, Derbyshire DE56 4EY (01332 842844)

The Hand and Heart
Nottingham

As well as medieval alabaster reliefs and the 'shrewd cash-chemistry' of the Boot family, Nottingham is noted for fine beer. Folk songs have been sung in its honour, the chorus of one assuring us that 'if she takes a glass often there's nothing can soften the heart of a woman like Nottingham ale'.

Not a sentiment that would pass unchallenged on the letters page of *The Guardian*, perhaps, but it was first voiced in less enlightened days, when the city's beer-some reputation depended on the sandstone caves beneath its pubs. These provided temperature-controlled cellarage in the days before electricity.

The Hand and Heart started trading in 1866, and is built into one such cave. An enticing view from the front bar discloses what appears to be a fairy-lit grotto. On closer inspection this turns out to be the former cellar, now serving as the restaurant area. Diners can rest assured that the sandstone is brushed twice a week to prevent gritty grains from falling into their confit duck or 'slow-braised' (as distinct from 'fast-braised', presumably) oxtail.

We choose to have lunch in the comparatively light and airy bar, where my more immediate concern is what to choose from no fewer than eight handpumps. Three more dispense ciders from the confines of the cave.

The beers are all from local-ish small breweries. Today they include Nottingham Dreadnought, a premium bitter with a robustly hoppy aftertaste. But the two regulars are Maypole Little Weed, a golden session ale brewed on a farm near Newark, and Round Heart from Dancing Duck, based sixteen miles up the road in Derby.

'It's well rounded,' the barmaid assures me. Mmm ... fruity too, I would suggest. It competes gamely with my lunch, rich red wine sauce swamping chunks of melt-in-the-mouth beef.

Tasty mushrooms and slivers of carrots occasionally bob up from the depths of the bowl, chased around by chunks of warm ciabatta bread. Sublime. My wife is equally enthusiastic about her soft yet densely flavoured belly pork in cider sauce.

Upstairs is the most exotic 'smoking terrace' I've come across since pubs and smouldering nubs parted company in 2006. And between the front bar and the fairy-lit cave is a piano that bursts into life every Sunday under the fingers, and sometimes the toes, of a pianist known as Pete the Feet.

Peering down at him from a photograph frame are two of the dray horses that delivered Shipstone's ales to the Hand and Heart when it was, believe me, a shadow of the pub it is today. Shippo's horses, renowned for their prodigious consumption, provided much steaming dung for local allotment holders. There was nothing could soften the bowels of a dray horse like Nottingham ale.

Chris Arnot, 17 January 2015

65–67 Derby Road, Nottingham NG1 5BA (0115 958 2456); thehandandheart.co.uk

The Robin Hood and Little John
Arnold, Nottinghamshire

A woman is rapping on the window of what is known in these parts as the 'beer-off' and elsewhere as the jug and bottle. Many pubs had them at one time. Customers, usually female, would arrive with a white jug to be filled up with draught ale and conveyed home to husbands or fathers – or whisked away for personal consumption.

This woman, however, only wants to borrow a set of stepladders. While her husband Mark obliges, Lorraine Swain, joint manager of the Robin Hood and Little John, is in the public bar pulling a pint of Marion Gold for a regular who has been for a long walk with his collie. Tongues are hanging out in both cases: one literally, the other metaphorically.

A bottled beer for dogs is on offer. It's called Snuffle and comes laced with chicken or beef stock. 'Council pop's good enough for her,' says her master. A bowl of water is laid on the bar's handsome slate floor and duly slurped.

The Marion is to be savoured rather than slurped. Pale yet full-bodied, it has a citrusy edge that goes perfectly with a chunk of pork pie, one of the *specialités de la maison*, along with ham 'cobs' and pickled eggs.

Marion shares the bar with a varying line-up of Merry Men-themed beers from the nearby Lincoln Green brewery: Hood bitter, a Tuck porter and Archer, an American-style IPA. Plus a couple of guest beers and the ever-reliable Everards' Tiger from over the Leicestershire border.

The perfectly balanced Hood rekindles memories of Home Bitter at its very best. Home Brewery was housed just up the road and its products were much in evidence around here until the company was swallowed by Scottish & Newcastle in 1986.

Mercifully, the only memory of the late-but-not-lamented S&N is resurrected by a startling tartan carpet in the lounge. Atop it is a piano that bursts into life for a sing-song every Wednesday.

As piano, pickled eggs and pork pie suggest, the Robin Hood and Little John is a shrine to the traditional street-corner 'boozer'. Except that it offers more. Much more. There are eight draught ciders, an espresso machine and a range of 44 whiskies from all over the place – Japan, India and even England.

And there's Big Ben mild, also from Lincoln Green, named after a local 19th-century bare-knuckle fighter, one Ben Gaunt, rather than a medieval outlaw. A hefty 6%, smooth and dark, it rolls over the tongue like liquid velvet, flattening any vinegary residue from a 'free-range and locally sourced' pickled egg that gives the impression that it hasn't spent several years in a jar – unlike its eye-wateringly acidic predecessors from the 'good old days' of street-corner boozers.

Chris Arnot, 6 June 2015

1 Church Street, Arnold, Nottinghamshire NG5 8FD (0115 920 1054); therobinhoodandlittlejohn.co.uk

The Dog and Bone
Lincoln

P ubs don't get more local than the Dog and Bone. This isn't some gigantic, city-centre boozorium, it's half a mile away from Lincoln's thronging High Street, along a road full of charity shops and student lodgings, then right at the butcher's shop on the corner. It sits nestled up to a line of small, terraced houses, and, once you're inside, turns out to be not much bigger than the neighbouring buildings.

Snug isn't just the word for the room you're in, it's a description of the atmosphere. There are stained-glass windows at the front door, local artists' pictures on the wall, and rows of well-filled bookshelves, which operate as a library. You walk on ancient, darkened floorboards, and sit on chairs enlivened by cushions bearing faces that look very much like the pub's resident dog.

The first thing that strikes you is how busy the blackboards are. Whereas most pubs make do with a monthly pub quiz, the Dog and Bone offers folk and rock jam sessions, plus roast lunch on the third Sunday of the month. Not to mention a burger night, a beer festival and a special sewing-and-gossiping night titled 'Stitch and Bitch'. And there are yet more plans, for a sports night and a pub walk.

All that plus free Wi-Fi, a Twitter address and an eccentric selection of decor from a pink coal scuttle to the antiquated wireless sets lining the top of the bar. No wonder it's the county's CAMRA Pub of the Year.

'It's hard work, but it's what people want,' says Sarah, the landlady, pulling a range of four different pints, and getting her husband, Chris, to disappear down the tiny trapdoor to find out what's wrong with the fifth.

After a bit of testing, and the pouring of a jug of froth down the basin, they decide the beer that's being difficult isn't up to the standard required, and withdraw it from the front line.

Which leaves challenging Wild Mule pale ale (from Roosters of Yorkshire, 3.0% ABV), Oldershaw Regal Blonde (golden, lager-like, 4.4%) and unusual Batemans Yella Belly Gold (golden, citrusy, 3.9%). Best by far, though, is Batemans XXXB (4.8%), as dark and rich as the wood panelling.

Step outside and you're in a small but cleverly laid-out garden (scrunchy stones, rather than grass), with ten leafy tables, one of them in a grapevine-covered gazebo. Plus there's a little, carriage-sized shed (The Kennel) to cope with overflow, due to either rain or customer numbers.

Sit out in the garden, and you can hear the great cathedral bell tolling from the top of the hill. To start with, you check your watch to see it's telling the right time, but after a while you stop taking any notice.

You may not actually be at home here, but it feels as if you are.

Christopher Middleton, 16 August 2014

10 John Street, Lincoln LN2 5BH (01522 522403); dogandbonelincoln.co.uk

The Little Mill Inn
Rowarth, Derbyshire

On my way to The Little Mill Inn I call in at Lyme Park, a National Trust property just a few miles away. There, I find a full-length portrait of a 17th-century gamekeeper, Joseph Watson. It is unusual to have a prominent portrait of a servant in such a house but this man was truly remarkable: he lived to the age of 105 and drank a gallon of beer every day.

You have to approach the Little Mill from the Cheshire side, because the roads simply end before reaching Derbyshire. The setting is stunning, with a riverside terrace overlooking a restored mill wheel on one side of the pretty white-painted pub. On the other side is a 70-foot 1932 railway carriage – the 'Derbyshire Belle', formerly of the Brighton Belle Railway, which was brought to the inn in 1978 by an eccentric landlord and which now has three en-suite bedrooms with original wood panelling and brass fittings. A red double-decker London bus also resides at the pub, bought by another enterprising landlord with the intention of getting customers there and returning them home at the end of the evening.

There has been a mill here since the turn of the 17th century, but the present structure dates from 1781, when it was established as a 'candlewick' mill, using the energy of the water to spin textiles. One landlord drowned in 1930, in a flash flood that also swept away the original mill wheel.

Inside there is an eclectic selection of locals at the bar and a homely atmosphere. You can hear the water running through the mill race. There are stone floors and wooden beams covered in horse brasses. A log fire crackles in the fireplace. There are gas-lamp-style wall lights and wooden settles. The friendly landlord stands behind the stone and wooden-beamed bar with its gleaming brass rail. There are hand-pulled beers including Hop and Under by Robinsons, a refreshing golden ale at 4.2%.

Banks's Bitter is malty and hoppy and 3.8%, and Jennings Bull's Eye (3.9%) is chestnut in colour and earthy and malty to taste. A draught cider, Hogan's Picker's Passion (5.3%), is also available.

An extensive menu is complemented by specials on a blackboard. Starters include deep-fried king prawns with sweet chilli and mixed leaves, and home-made chicken liver pâté with herbed bread. Main courses that draw the eye include local pork and leek sausages with creamy mash. From the specials board, however, local Rowarth shin of beef in red wine gravy on horseradish mash is simply wonderful.

There is an extensive wine list; live music at weekends comes from bands with names like the Squirrelkickers and Down Fall Band.

Ed Jowsey, 24 October 2015

Rowarth, High Peak, Derbyshire SK22 1EB (01663 743178); thelittlemill.co.uk; approach via Marple Bridge

The Angler's Rest
Bamford, Derbyshire

The Angler's Rest in Bamford, in the Peak District, is one of more than 36 community pubs in the UK. As 29 pubs a week close across the country – nearly half of those in villages – there is a growing movement to protect these valuable community assets.

The Angler's Rest was a farm that brewed and served beer, becoming a staging inn in the 19th century. It declined under the management of a Pubco and, after a succession of short-term tenants and little investment, was about to close. In 2013 it was purchased by more than 300 shareholders and is now run for the benefit of the community as the Angler's Pub, the Rest Café and Bamford Post Office and Bunkhouse.

On this Friday evening it is frequented by a cluster of locals at the bar and various groupuscules here and there. A peloton of middle-aged cyclists comes in. They sit with their beers, Lycra'd haunches squeaking on the leather armchairs in the carpeted midsection of the pub. A young farmer at the bar is wearing a T-shirt that declares that 'Happiness is a New Tractor and a Girlfriend' – presumably in that order. The atmosphere is lively and comfortable as landlady Amanda lets me try some of the ales before I select a refreshing pint of Brampton Brewery Griffin Pale Ale (4.1%) – summery, malty and slightly sweet.

Amanda is rightly proud of the community pub and happy to point out its merits while engaging in banter with the locals.

Other beers on offer are the strangely named Dukeries

Brewery De Lovetot (4.2%) which has a citrus taste; Intrepid's Explorer (4.0%), a local blonde ale; Great Heck's very fruity Citra (4.5%) and Black Sheep (3.8%).

I find a table in a more austere area, before ordering a baked camembert to share. It comes with an excellent salad incorporating samphire, surprisingly. Given that we're about as far from the coast as you can get, the samphire is obviously the exception that proves the rule of locally sourced ingredients that's generally in force. Indeed, my waitress Daisy is herself locally sourced – her parents are shareholders.

For our main course we choose crispy confit of duck and vegetarian chilli nachos – both excellent.

There is a pool table and upright piano as if to emphasise that the pub serves all of the community. Wednesday night is pie-and-quiz night and there is a farmers' market every third Saturday.

If your local is under threat, you could apply to register it as an Asset of Community Value, a first step towards making it a community pub like this one. Help is available from The Pub is The Hub and The Plunkett Foundation, which can be found online.

Ed Jowsey, 5 September 2015

Main Road, Bamford, Derbyshire S33 0DY (01433 659317); www.anglers.rest

Yorkshire & Humberside

The Kelham Island
Sheffield

There are Chinese palm trees in the beer garden.
Indian bean trees, Chilean climbers and bamboo,
too. Statues of Hindu and Buddhist gods are peering
through the foliage. Welcome to Kelham Island – or, more
specifically, The Kelham Island.

No wonder the pub attracts what owner Trevor Wraith
calls 'Oriental visitors', brought here by employees of
nearby HSBC bank. Be they from Hong Kong, Shanghai or
even Canary Wharf, they may well be pleasantly surprised
to find such a verdant oasis amid the dereliction of post-
industrial Sheffield, where demolition men are still cutting
a swathe through former cutlery and scissor-making
factories.

Outside a back lounge thronged with young bank
workers is a lamp advertising Ward's, once the cutlers' beer
of choice. The brewery was swallowed up and closed down
in 1999. But, fifteen years on, there are more than enough
replacements and this, the venue voted CAMRA's national
pub of the year in 2008 and 2009, is as good a place as any
to sample a few.

On a handsomely carved wooden bar surrounded by
distinctive red and white tiles are no fewer than thirteen
real ales, most of which are unknown to me.

One exception is Bradfield Farmer's Blonde, with
which I had a brief dalliance in Chesterfield last summer.
Deception, brewed by Abbeydale elsewhere in Sheffield,
seems an ungrateful response to her seductive charms. It
turns out to be equally pale and aromatic, and the bitter

taste that it leaves in the mouth is refreshing rather than astringently regretful.

Acorn Barnsley Bitter is almost chestnut brown, more complex and well rounded. There are also stouts and milds and powerful porters, some weighing in at 6% or 7% ABV. Acorn's Old Moor Porter may be a mere 4.4%, but it's hefty enough to compete with the thick, rich gravy and melt-in-the-mouth meat of a boeuf bourguignon par excellence.

It comes with peas and delicious chips that stay crisp when surreptitiously dipped. A more than satisfying six-quid's worth.

The pub's enormous ginger cat has grown fat on a diet of pork scratchings and biltong. Pussycat, as she's known, is unaccountably missing this lunchtime from her usual stool near a fireplace topped by an Edwardian mantel clock and two china dogs.

In that corner of the bar sit what look like long-standing regulars, including a bald man in a waistcoat with a watch chain worthy of an alderman. He is holding what appears to be a decent crib hand close to his chest. On closer inspection, he is looking at his smartphone. So are all the other venerable figures around the table. Tweeting, or virtual dominoes? Post-industrial Sheffield is full of surprises.

Chris Arnot, 9 August 2014

62 Russell Street, Sheffield S3 8RW (0114 272 2482); kelhamtavern.co.uk

The Rat and Ratchet
Huddersfield

The lunchtime menu is hardly extensive. You can have pork pie, pork pie, crisps or pork pie. Proper Yorkshire pork pie, mind you, made by a local butcher with a penetrable crust, a minimum of jelly and meat that is pink rather than grey in the middle. This is Huddersfield, not Melton Mowbray.

There will be bread and dripping on the bar later, a treat for the taste buds, if not the arteries.

'I put out two plates of it, piled high, during the interval on quiz night and it's all gone before we start the next round,' says the landlord Richard Prest, who seems glad to be back in his native Yorkshire after years of exile in the south.

The Rat and Ratchet is a no-nonsense alehouse with several drinking areas, a dart board, a high-backed settle or two, exposed floorboards and a central island of impressive black-and-white tiles topped by a vintage jukebox and the sort of pinball machine that I last saw in a students' union in the days before decimal currency.

Beyond the window are distant hills and redundant mills with soot-encrusted chimneys. And between here and there are several lanes of traffic.

While waiting for the lights to change, some drivers have been alarmed to see steam rising from the grate on the pavement outside. Whence the sign on the outside wall of local stone: 'We are brewing. The building is not on fire.' The fire brigade once came close to breaking down the door when the pub was closed, having been alerted by the hoppy clouds rising from the mash tuns in the cellar below.

Vegetarians may find the Rat and Ratchet not to their taste, but for connoisseurs of fine beer it's worth truffling out.

This is one of three micro-outposts of the Ossett Brewery, and its impressive range is well represented. The biggest seller by far is White Rat, pale yet heavily hopped, and 4% ABV. Brewed on the premises, it's yours for £2.40 a pint. Despite its name, the Pure Gold is more of an amber ale, beautifully balanced, slightly lower on alcohol (3.8%) yet just as flavoursome.

There's a powerful porter, a stout given depth and intensity by black treacle, a German Weissbier and much more.

A solitary pump serves cider, but many more varieties are fetched up those well-worn cellar steps on request. Udders Orchard is made by the previous landlord who collects his raw materials from gardens in the locality like a Tyke-ish Eddie Grundy.

Let's face it, alcoholic apple juice is as close as you're going to get to fruit and veg in this place.

Chris Arnot, 1 March 2014

40 Chapel Hill, Huddersfield HD1 3EB (01484 542400);
ossett-brewery.co.uk/pubs/rat-and-ratchet-huddersfield

The Booth Wood Inn
Rishworth, West Yorkshire

The Oldham to Ripponden Turnpike, a trans-Pennine, Lancashire–Yorkshire highway, opened in 1795. Entrepreneurs took note and in no time at all alehouses sprang up along the route – including the Booth Wood Inn. If you were travelling from Oldham, on foot, on horseback or by stagecoach, then the worst part of the journey, over rough, bleak, open moorland, was over by the time you reached Rishworth. It must have been a relief – the weather up here can be brutal.

By the 1840s, the pub, for obvious reasons, was known as the Coach and Horses. In the 1850s, it was the Oddfellows' Arms, and in the 1880s the Cunning Corner (it is on a dangerous bend in the road). This century it became the Old Bore (what was all that about?) and a couple of years ago things came full circle and it was the Booth Wood Inn again.

The bar offers a handsome variety of drinks – in moderation, of course. There is a double shelf full of my favourite malt whiskies, a latticework behind the bar is packed with wine bottles, with prices by the glass or bottle chalked everywhere. Last but not least, half a dozen handpumps stand sentinel along the bar. The landlord's brother runs a microbrewery in Halifax, so naturally, you will see Oates' beers featuring strongly. I'm working my way through the list and can thoroughly recommend Summit (4.5%), which has a real kick of hops to it, and OMT, or Oates Mean Time (3.8%), a lemony refresher.

Sorting out food requires a bit of legwork. There is a

printed menu, a list of specials on a chalkboard at the end of the room on the left, and another chalkboard with what's called the 'Retro' menu to the right of the main bar.

'Retro,' said someone or other, 'is nostalgia with a dose of cynicism and detachment.' How can you possibly feel cynical or detached about fish, chips and mushy peas, or pork kebabs with tzatziki and salad at £5 the plate? On the other hand, the specials one day did include pork belly, black pudding bon bon, leeks, kale, onions, with cider sauce, which was magnificent and great value at £12.15.

Outside, a pleasant small beer garden is surrounded by flower boxes and decorated with a purple bicycle – memories linger of the Tour de France, or the Tour de Yorkshire as it was known here. You can see sheep safely grazing on the lower slopes opposite. Higher up, on the shoulder of the moor, you can make out a section of the latest Pennine crossing, the M62, with an unending nose-to-tail line of traffic. Today, at least, you can give thanks for being down here and not up there.

Arthur Taylor, 21 March 2015

Oldham Road, Rishworth, Halifax, West Yorkshire HX6 4QU (01422 825600); boothwoodinn.co.uk

The Robin Hood Inn
Cragg Vale, West Yorkshire

The Cragg Vale road begins in the Calder Valley at Mytholmroyd, Yorkshire, and climbs through woods and houses to the moorlands around Blackstone Edge, Lancashire. At the lower end, there's a blue notice which announces that the route is 5.5 miles long, climbs 968 feet and is the 'longest continuous gradient in England'. Cyclists regard it as a challenge and every time you drive along it, there they are, exhibiting rictus-grins of pain for pleasure.

The Robin Hood, a sturdy building of millstone grit and Yorkshire slate, is a mile or so out of Mytholmroyd. There's a sign, featuring the man himself and a cast-iron can't fail invitation:

'Ye Bowmen and ye Archers good, Come in and drink with Robin Hood. If Robin to the fete has gone, Then take a glass with Little John.'

You are in the cosy, small, higgledy-piggledy main room as soon as you set foot in the place. There's a lovely Victorian fireplace with a coal and log fire always ablaze. I call this bar the gossip zone, because I find I'm usually drawn into conversation before I even sit down. The Robin, as it is known hereabout, is a locals' pub.

There are three cask beers on offer, two of them, left and right, Landlord and Golden Best, from the Timothy Taylor brewery in Keighley. The centre pump is for a guest beer, which changes regularly. The locals like to try the new beer, so the order is often 'two pints from the middle, please'.

The pub is run by Roger and Elva Wood, who are

farmers, so the beef for the burgers (£6.50 with chips and salad) or the lamb (£13.50 lamb shoulder with rosemary and red wine gravy, plus a mountain of vegetables) come from animals last seen grazing the fields behind the pub.

The huge talking point in the Robin at the moment is the 2014 Tour de France. On the second day, 6 July, on a 200-kilometre run from York to Sheffield, the peloton will travel right past the front door of the pub, tackling that famous incline. 'I reckon we'll have a lock-in that day,' chortles one of the regulars.

Arthur Taylor, 29 June 2013

Cragg Road, Cragg Vale, Hebden Bridge, West Yorkshire HX7 5SQ (01422 885899); Mon–Wed, 3pm–midnight; Thu–Sun, noon–midnight

The Staff of Life
Todmorden, West Yorkshire

The Staff of Life is a mile or so out of Todmorden, up the Burnley Road, a long and winding way with high wooded hills topped by crags on either side. The pub car park, the only place to stop on what is a very dangerous road, is on the right, about 100 yards short of the place itself. First-timers usually miss the car park, spot the pub, curse, then have to drive miles up the road to find somewhere to turn, being closely pursued the while by impatient lorry drivers and white-van men.

The stroll from the car park gives time to savour the view, with Eagle's Crag jutting dramatically over the skyline and thundering streams of water cascading down the hillside through the trees into the River Calder.

A stride through the door brings you to a semi-circular snug bar, with a table and chairs under the window and stools around the bar for drinkers. The *Todmorden News*, essential reading for local news and scandal, is usually strewn about on a seat here.

A couple of Timothy Taylor's beers, Landlord and Boltmaker, are always available. Guest beers on offer are all local or regional and are tended with loving care and attention. The rest of the pub, all flag floors, wooden beams, exposed stone and wooden panelling, is rather like a multiple cave. The room at the back, up some stone stairs and under a dangerously low head-banging lintel, has work by local artists on the walls. If you choose to sit up here, you get a fine overview of the rest of the customers.

The Staff is primarily a diners' pub, albeit diners with

a taste for cask ale. If you want to eat on Friday evening, Saturday or Sunday, it's a good idea to book. We tried the seafood meze (£12), which is served on a plank for two, with Morecambe Bay shrimps, tempura king prawns, smoked salmon, smoked mackerel pâté and salad. Porcus sausages (and mash £10.50) come from the farm on the hill opposite.

You might come across the local beekeepers' association, Todmorden Harriers, the cricket club and others who meet here. Wednesday night is quiz night, the first Monday of the month is the knitting club. This latter activity seems to be happening all over the place. Is knitting the new darts?

Arthur Taylor, 9 February 2013

550 Burnley Road, Lydgate, Todmorden, West Yorkshire OL14 8JF (01706 819033); staffoflifeinn.org.uk

The White Lion
Heptonstall, West Yorkshire

Make sure you are in peak condition for your visit to Heptonstall. Towngate, the narrow main road, is steep – lung-burstingly steep going up, and knee-crackingly steep going down.

The White Lion, two-thirds of the way up, is worth the effort. Most days, you want the small cosy main bar, which has a huge stone fireplace, above which is inscribed 'Time is Precious. Waste it Wisely'.

On sunny days, it's probably better to head for the beer garden at the back. If it is sunny but chilly, a common weather pattern hereabout, they have blankets you can borrow, free of charge, to stay wrapped up outside.

The mainly regional cask beers are presented with educational aids. Each one of the six pumps has a small clear glass jar in front of it, filled with the beer in question, so you can admire the colour. There's a chalkboard, which lists the said beers, together with their breweries, relative strengths and colours. They have one-third size glasses, so you can taste three beers to the pint.

My initial experiment included Chinook 4.2% ABV, a blonde beer from the Goose Eye Brewery, Keighley. Chinook is a hop, by the way, not a helicopter. I sipped two beers from the Saltaire Brewery, Pride, another blonde at 3.9% and Cascadian Black (guess the colour?) at a dangerous 4.8%.

There's a gin of the week – today it's Bombay Sapphire with apple and summer berries, £2.75. Next to it, the malt of the week – The BenRiach, Speyside. Round the side of the bar there's a note that this week's cider is 'Stinger', with guarana, a natural pick-me-up.

Pub visits are always instructive – I had never heard of guarana, so looked it up when I got home. Brazilian, it seems, with a nasty mythology.

I gave the slip to all these temptations and went for a pint of Saltaire Pride, having decided that this was the best of the three tasters to go with my north Indian goat curry, with rice and garlic and coriander naan bread.

Yorkshire folk, in my experience, can put away enormous amounts of food without even trying. Once when I was here, I went for the sausage and mash (£8.95), which was a truly mountainous portion. I cleared the delicious local sausages, but, shamefaced, had to leave most of the mash, some of the cabbage and a few carrots. The White Lion wisely offers half portions of most things for lesser mortals. My mini-curry cost a mere £4.95 and was plenty.

The place mats bear quotations from the poets Sylvia Plath and Ted Hughes. They knew the village well. Sylvia is a permanent resident – her much-visited grave is in the churchyard.

Arthur Taylor, 21 November 2015

58 Towngate, Heptonstall, West Yorkshire HX7 7NB (01422 842027); facebook.com/whitelion.heptonstall

The Adelphi Hotel
Leeds

The Adelphi bears testimony to the resilience, as well as the opulence and flamboyance, of late-Victorian architecture. Built a dozen years before the *Titanic*, its frontage comes to a head like the prow of a particularly tall and majestic liner that's rather too big to set sail on the nearby River Aire.

Inside is a cornucopia of colourful tiles and carved mahogany, etched glass and polished brass. Polished walnut, too, gleams across the floor of one of four downstairs rooms as well as the imposing function room upstairs. It's accessed via a broad and lavishly tiled staircase rising majestically from a passageway sporting a bar with a row of handpumps.

The products of Joshua Tetley and Son would have gushed from each of them at one time. Tetley workers gathered at the Adelphi every evening to continue sampling the fruits of their labours with the draymen who humped 36-gallon barrels of the stuff down cellar steps. They were renowned for their prodigious consumption, as indeed were the dray horses that regularly found their way home to their stables with some fourteen pints under their bridles.

The last horse was put out to grass at the turn of the (21st) century and the brewery closed in 2011. Tetley's is now brewed in Wolverhampton. The biggest brewery in Leeds today is the one named after the city. Leeds Pale is a regular at the Adelphi. A light and hoppy session beer, it nonetheless has a lingering bitter finish that provides a satisfying accompaniment to my suitably gloopy and full-flavoured farro, mushroom, roast butternut squash and truffle risotto: not your standard pub grub, I'll grant you – and not cheap either at £10.50.

Even the sandwiches are around the £6.50–£7 mark, but appear to be considerably more imaginative than your average ham or cheese. There's a New-York-deli-style offering, including pastrami and sauerkraut, as well as a buffalo mozzarella, tomato, spinach and crème fraîche. On focaccia, if you please. And you can have bacon with that for an additional £1.25.

The menu is evidently targeted at a new breed of regulars, as indeed is the extensive range of Belgian, German and American keg and bottled beers. Goodbye brewery workers and hello to those who ply their trade in the digital media, marketing and finance companies hereabout.

It's comparatively quiet on a Monday lunchtime in the onetime 'tap room' where there's a fascinating conversation under way on the nocturnal habits of hamsters and guinea pigs. The clock mounted on an elaborately carved bar-back has stopped at twenty to ten. Who knows in which year – or, indeed, in which century?

For all the recent changes at the Adelphi, the surroundings still give the impression that time has stood still.

Chris Arnot, 25 October 2014

1–3 Hunslet Road, Leeds LS10 1JQ (0113 245 6377); theadelphileeds.co.uk

The Fleece
Otley, West Yorkshire

O tley is an attractive, quirky market town in Lower Wharfedale. You have to warm to a place that supports five morris dancing teams, a brass band and a ukulele orchestra, not to mention annual agricultural shows, walking, folk and beer festivals. There's a Beer Club too, which keeps an eye on all the town's seventeen pubs.

The Fleece doesn't reveal its true glory until you get around to the back and see the view – a fine terraced garden, descending steeply to the river, with woods, fields and rolling hills in the background beyond. Inside, you can admire the fruits of a total refurbishment a couple of years ago.

There's a large dining area – tables with windows overlooking the famous view tend to fill up fast. The menu is written up on a huge slate wall by the bar. There's something for everyone, and every dish is beautifully presented. I remember working with a cameraman who, if he was in a good mood, would snap the machine off at the end of a day's shoot and declare, beaming, 'Every frame a Rembrandt.' Every plate is a bit like that.

I went for 'Holy Cow', ox cheeks and red wine with chilli chips and fresh garden peas (£10.50). My wife, a conservative soul sometimes, had roast mackerel, with lemon capers and herby new potatoes (£10). We shared a cheese board – four cheeses, two of them local, a dollop of home-made chutney and a bunch of grapes, the lot wreathed in a swag of watercress, presented on a slab of slate (£8).

The Fleece is owned by the WharfeBank Brewery, which is only a couple of miles downstream. Naturally, their beers figure prominently: at least seven or eight of them at the latest count. The excellent barmaid described all of them, then suggested Verbeia Pale Ale, a light gold refreshing beer, for our meal. Verbeia was the goddess of the River Wharfe, she confided. Nice to know these things. She was right – it was a fine choice.

For me, the best room in the whole place is the snug ('Dogs and Wellies welcome'), a loving recreation of a traditional tap room, with red-tile floor, leather-backed seating and, wonder of wonders, a couple of highly polished domino tables, real antiques, with ridges around the sides to stop over-enthusiastically shovelled tiles falling to the floor, and a shelf underneath to stow your pints while you take your turn.

Here we retired after eating, for a pint of Tether Blond – absolute contentment. I congratulated the barmaid's male colleague on the décor. 'Aye,' he said, 'it will look just about right when it's had ten years or so to get properly worn in.' Very wise young man, that.

Arthur Taylor, 25 May 2013

Westgate, Otley, West Yorkshire LS21 3DT (01943 465034); fleece-otley.wix.com/fleece-otley

The Craven Arms
Appletreewick, North Yorkshire

Most Yorkshire Dales run west to east, but scenic Wharfedale meanders roughly north to south. As it does so, it runs close by The Craven Arms. Craven is the name of Sir William Craven (1548–1614) who was born in Appletreewick and has subsequently become known as 'The Yorkshire Dick Whittington' after making his fortune and becoming mayor of London. His good works can be seen in the churches and bridges of the area.

The Craven Arms also dates back to the 16th century and has retained its original features, such as beamed ceilings, stone floors and a big stone fireplace around a cast-iron range and log fire. There are wooden tables, gas lamps (yes, really) and church pew seats. A dart board sits disconcertingly above a dining table (presumably this is moved when a darts match takes place). The owners are David and Robert Aynesworth and the staff are local, as is much of the fare.

The unique feature of this pub, however, is its amazing cruck barn, completed in 2006 and the first to be constructed in the dale for over 300 years. A door to the right of the bar takes you along a short corridor and up a few steps into the barn. A cruck barn has an A-frame of unseasoned oak which contorts as it dries to give a character not possible with modern building methods. Local materials have been used to provide an authentic feel – insulation is sheep wool (treated to make it fire resistant) and the walls are local stone and lime and horsehair plaster.

The cruck barn is generally used as a restaurant, but can be hired for special events. A sign in the bar advertises suitably old-school sporting contests and live music from acoustic performers including a Yorkshire folk singer whose repertoire includes the appropriate Beer Belly Blues.

There are eight cask-conditioned real ales to choose from in the bar including Thwaites' Wainwright, a golden light ale with subtle hoppy flavours. There are several from Hetton's Dark Horse Brewery including the specially brewed Cruck Barn Bitter. I chose this one and was rewarded with a crisp traditional bitter that stayed bright and had malty overtones. The menu on a chalk board in the bar is locally sourced and has a number of game dishes as well as pub classics such as mixed grill and fish and chips. I decided on the wild boar and venison casserole, which was sublime.

There is a beer garden with fine views of the dales. Even the gents washroom is interesting, with pictures of inspirational people such as Nelson Mandela and John Lennon. This may well be the perfect country pub with its mixture of history and great food and drink in a friendly atmosphere.

Ed Jowsey, 10 January 2015

Appletreewick, Skipton, North Yorkshire BD23 6DA (01756 720270); craven-cruckbarn.co.uk

Hales' Bar
Harrogate, North Yorkshire

Harrogate's image is as staid and steady as a silver pot on a marble tabletop in Bettys. But stroll down the street at the side of those fabled tea rooms, circumnavigate the vast bulk of the Crown Hotel, and you come across a venue altogether more quirky and unpredictable.

Hales' Bar is named after William Hales, who became the landlord in 1882, and the saloon bar can have changed little since his day. Lighting is still provided by gas mantles. Smoke no longer swirls beneath them, but sharing the bar with six handpumps are two ornate brass cigar lighters that flare like Bunsen burners on impact with a naked flame.

Behind the bar, above huge barrels that might once have dispensed amontillados in Yates's Wine Lodges, are cases full of stuffed birds. There may well be a great auk or bustard among them; it's difficult to tell in this light. One case, mind you, is occupied by an exhibit rarely seen in municipal museums – a scale model of Tweety Pie.

Amanda Wilkinson, the William Hales *de nos jours*, has a mischievous sense of humour. She also loves a party, and so do her regulars. Last time I was here, after a day at the Scarborough Cricket Festival, I spotted a piano through the gaslit glow – a fortuitous find in the circumstances.

I'd been chatting to a visitor from Devon who turned out to be a cocktail-bar pianist. He promptly sat down at the keyboard and regaled us with everything from boogie-woogie to *My Bonnie Lies Over the Ocean*. The clientele responded by singing along and, in some cases, dancing the night away.

Having arrived too late to sample the evening menu (steaks and ribs served on cast-iron skillets a speciality), I returned on a much chillier day to try one of the homely lunchtime dishes. The meat in the steak pie was melt-in-the-mouth flavoursome and the piping jug of rich, glutinous gravy softened the pastry without turning the chips soggy.

A man warming his hands on a cigar lighter confided that the Bass was the best he'd had since he left Burton-on-Trent. But I can get Bass in my local. What I can't get is an Old Leg Over.

It's sited next to the Dizzy Blonde on this bar lined with brassy taps and priapic pumps. The Blonde is young and zesty, the Leg Over a slightly nutty 4.1% beer brewed by Daleside in Harrogate. Both are in tip-top condition, as is Daleside's Hales' Ale, a clean-tasting amber session bitter.

William Hales is catching up with the eponymous Betty. He now has a beer as well as a bar named after him.

Chris Arnot, 16 November 2013

1–3 Crescent Road, Harrogate, North Yorkshire HG1 2RS (01423 725570); halesbar.co.uk; food served every lunchtime from noon–2.30pm and evenings from 5–8pm except Sun and Mon

The Three-Legged Mare
York

If you were around in the 16th century and heading for a three-legged mare, you'd have been in for a spot of bother. The horizontal wooden triangular structure was a form of execution used to terminal effect at Tyburn in London from 1571.

The contemporary pub in York sharing the name is a much more welcoming prospect, however. It's one of three owned by York Brewery in a city not short of excellent pubs. The Three-Legged Mare features nine real ale hand-pulls; six from the mother ship brewed within the city walls and three 'guests', plus a selection of bottled 'world' beers.

York Brewery enjoys a well-earned reputation and although our first notebook entries are hieroglyphics representing high-backed pew seating, a spiral staircase and a red piano, it's Yorkshire Terrier (4.2% ABV) that deserves particular acknowledgement. It's an outstanding ale with a touch of malt on the palate complemented by a lazily insistent citrus orange hop sensation in each mouthful.

Others on the bar include the dark ruby Centurion's Ghost (5.4% ABV), Guzzler (3.6% ABV) and a couple from Tring in Hertfordshire. A tray of four, one-third pints is a novel way of taking the city tour.

Seating areas in the Three-Legged Mare (known locally as the Wonky Donkey) have been cleverly thought out, making good use of the pub's available space, and high rear windows revealing a conservatory-style room and pleasant beer garden – complete with model scaffold –

create a degree of visual elbow room. It is more continental café-bar than traditional city-centre boozer in style, and it manages to straddle the one-off tourist trade and the regular visitor with ease.

This could be down to some sort of Yorkshire 'terroir', a combination of factors leading to a satisfactory conclusion. For example, the staff appear to know all there is to know about beer, someone will strike up conversation, a sense of humour prevails with a chalkboard pub prayer – 'Forgive us our spillages, as we forgive those who spill against us' – while the red piano and zipped-up double bass in the corner simply ache for impromptu sessions.

And are those aluminium casks waiting to be collected, or connected to the pumps, or are they part of the furnishings? If they are décor that also does a job, that is a good thing, as function should come alongside fashion in a pub that is serious about its beer.

Three-legged mare executions were mass spectator events and a crowd of thousands was attracted to Tyburn in 1649 to witness 23 men and one woman hanged simultaneously. A red piano may not have that allure, but a Yorkshire terrier is unfailingly fetching.

Alastair Gilmour, 12 July 2014

15 High Petergate, York YO1 7EN (01904 638246); york-brewery.co.uk/Pubs/The-Three-Legged-Mare

The Golden Fleece
York

There is a skeleton sitting at the bar next to me as I order a pint of Timothy Taylor's Landlord (4.3%). He already has a drink so I don't offer to buy him one – and anyway he doesn't look like he can hold his liquor. His name, it seems, is Saul Goodfellow and he even has his own blog.

The Golden Fleece claims to be York's most haunted pub. Here in the back, or Merchant's Bar, there are gas lamps and the low-beamed ceiling is painted dark red. The chairs and tables are dark wood on wooden floorboards, making it seem very dark indeed.

From the outside the Golden Fleece is a quaint, narrow, slightly crooked building dating back to 1503 and squashed between two larger oak-beamed neighbours opposite the celebrated Shambles row of medieval shops in the centre of York. A ghostly white cat protrudes from the wall above the pub sign, probably put there to ward off rats and mice in the past. The pub was named for guild members of the nearby Merchant Adventurers' Hall who used to trade in fleeces and wool. Their own building on Fossgate is a masterpiece and well worth a visit.

Inside the Fleece, the front bar is bright and sparsely furnished and the barman is friendly and welcoming. A narrow corridor leads through to the back bar and the beer garden. In the corridor a series of white death masks are mounted on shields adding to the spooky atmosphere. There are regular live music nights in the Merchant's Bar and there are four letting rooms, from £100 per night, all with free ghosts it seems.

Other beers on the hand-pulls at the bar are Wychwood's Hobgoblin (at 4.5%), Theakston's Old Peculier (5.6%), Skipton's Copper Dragon Best Bitter (3.8%), Theakston's Best Bitter (3.8%) and Freedom Organic English Lager (4.8%).

The menu is comprehensive with a variety of sandwiches and jacket potatoes from £5.95, chicken curry (£8.95), moules with crusty bread (£9.95).

Apparently there are five resident ghosts, including Lady Alice Peckett whose husband, John, owned the pub and was Lord Mayor of York in 1702. One-eyed Jack is a 17th-century ghost with a flintlock pistol and there is a Canadian airman reputed to have fallen from the third floor after a drinking session during the war. The hangman William 'Mutton' Curry used to drink in the pub.

For a time, the bodies of convicted criminals hanged nearby would be stored in the cellar until claimed by their relatives – and the cellar is the scene of many ghostly appearances. A metal plate on the door warns 'Beware of the Ghosts' and a phantom-themed walk entitled the York Terror Trail starts from here every evening.

I have another drink with Saul the skeleton and thankfully, the only spirits I see are in the optics behind the bar.

Ed Jowsey, 18 July 2015

16 Pavement, York YO1 9UP (01904 625171); thegoldenfleeceyork.co.uk

The Cross Keys
Thixendale, North Yorkshire

I t's an unexpected place to find a pub, never mind a
thriving one. Thixendale is an isolated hamlet of maybe
two dozen houses tucked into a deep niche of the Yorkshire
Wolds. At the spectacular confluence of six valleys – David
Hockney has repeatedly painted three adjacent trees in one
of them – it takes some finding whether you arrive by car
or, as many do, by foot.

Behind a white façade as simple as a child's drawing
– four windows with a door in the middle – the single,
L-shaped room of the Cross Keys is a convenient resting
point for hardy souls stalking the 79-mile Wolds Way.

Dating from at least 1851, the pub lures a sprinkling of
patrons at lunchtime (Thursday to Sunday only), but on
a recent Saturday it was thronged. The first warm day of
the year coincided with the Woldsman, a 50-mile saunter
organised by the Long Distance Walkers' Association
(LDWA).

A mixture of LDWA members and less energetic visitors
slaked their thirsts with resident Tetley's Cask (3.7% ABV)
and guests Copper Dragon Golden Pippin (3.9% ABV)
and Jennings Bitter (3.5% ABV). As might be expected at
Yorkshire CAMRA's 2012 Pub of the Season, they were in
good nick.

Negotiating the ruddy-faced striders, we squeezed
around the sole remaining table. Our neighbour, a young
woman who was 'only doing an eight-mile circular', stared
at her great plate of chilli con carne (£5.50) fringed by a
halo of buttered pitta bread. 'Masses, isn't it?' she said, but

minutes later her plate was clean.

My wife went for a robust chestnut casserole (£6.25) while I had a pleasingly juicy steak and Guinness pie (£7.45) accompanied by a choice of peas ('garden or mushy?') and a hillock of chips. 'These are walkers' quantities,' I blurted to the landlord, Steve Anstey.

'No, just Yorkshire,' he replied.

He conceded, however, that the menu was tailored to walkers' requirements.

'When we took over the pub 27 years ago, we started with healthy food and got it wrong. Walkers want something cheap and cheerful to fill them up.'

Those not engaged in a long-distance trek may prefer the sandwiches, generously filled with cheese (£3.55) or roast beef and ham (£4.25).

The need to refuel does not mean that walkers lack discrimination. Today, much of their conversation revolved around food. The mere mention of the Welsh rarebit served at the Ramblers' Rest Café in Millington provoked sighs of delight from three adjoining tables. With closing time approaching (the pub shuts from 3–6pm), boots were laced and backpacks hoisted into place. 'Enjoy the next 25 miles.'

'Thanks. I've got to finish by 4am.' It was a less demanding journey to see Mr Hockney's oaks, especially by car.

Christopher Hirst, 27 April 2013

Thixendale, Malton, North Yorkshire YO17 9TG (01377 288272)

The Lion Inn
Blakey Ridge, North Yorkshire

B lakey Ridge is a bleak grouse moor with breathtaking views over Rosedale and Farndale in the heart of the North Yorkshire Moors. Standing atop it at 1,312 feet above sea level, the Lion Inn is isolated and frequently cut off in winter. Apparently, when it starts to snow people come from miles around hoping to be snowed in. In 2010 it was nine days before the snowploughs got through – that's quite a lock-in.

Built in 1553 by monks who transported coffins across the moors to Whitby Abbey, the Lion has thick stone walls and considerable history. It was a farmers' market for Danby and Fryup Dale in the 18th century, and it boomed in the 19th and early 20th centuries, when iron-ore mining was the biggest employer in the area. Now tourists and walkers seek shelter from the unforgiving landscape, and on a sunny spring day there are bound to be huddles of coast-to-coast hikers sampling the seven real ales on offer in the bar rooms.

Most popular – especially with Americans – is Theakston's Old Peculier (5.6%), which is dark and has a deep, sweet flavour. There is also Theakston's Best Bitter (3.8%), Thwaites Wainwright (4.1%), Skipton Copper Dragon (4.0%), Black Sheep (4.4%) and Thwaites Original (3.6%) on offer – so I am spoilt for choice.

The free house is now run by the Crossland family. It is warm and friendly: huge inside, with six separate bar rooms and restaurants, but somehow still cosy. There are rustic wooden doors which are dangerously low. The restaurant rooms have red velvet chairs and red tablecloths, wooden settles and an old grandfather clock. By the huge stone fireplace in one of the bar rooms there is a grand piano surrounded by a variety of historic pictures and one photograph of the inn almost buried in snow.

The menu is hearty enough, and the portions large enough, to refuel the most energetic hill-climber. There are steaks, pies, burgers and more exotic offerings on a specials blackboard. The Old Peculier casserole is tempting, as is the chef's own chicken curry, but lunch for me is a jacket potato with a really good chilli.

A group of American women in walking gear are enthusing about the beer and the chips. They look to have settled in with no thoughts of walking further today. There are ten letting rooms for coast-to-coast walkers to rest up and this must be a high point of that long-distance path in more ways than one.

As I zip up my coat before continuing my walk towards the North Sea, I am sorely tempted to rejoin the Americans by the fire with their pints of Old Peculier, and their enthusiasm for all things old and British.

Ed Jowsey, 20 June 2015

Blakey Ridge, Kirkbymoorside, North Yorkshire YO62 7LQ
(01751 417320); lionblakey.co.uk

The White Bear Hotel
Masham, North Yorkshire

The steam billowing over the White Bear's rooftop is heady with malted barley. It's an aromatic appetiser promising flavourful beer to come, but there's a catch.

We're breathing deeply on Black Sheep ale from the brewery behind, while the pub is the 'tap' for T&R Theakston whose own brewery lies a short walk away – and the two were once bitter rivals in a civil war that followed takeover after takeover and a deep family rift in 1992, when one disillusioned Theakston upped and founded Black Sheep.

The Theakstons may have crossed swords for a few years but happily the extended family now works amicably in tandem, promoting Masham's unique position in brewing folklore.

The White Bear's two bars bristle with Theakston's hand-pulls: Black Bull Bitter, Hogshead Bitter, Golden Lightfoot and Old Peculier, a strong, dark and complex beer with a dash of independent spirit – a 'peculier' is a parish outside the jurisdiction of a diocese.

The original White Bear was flattened by a German bomber in 1941, en route from a raid on Belfast, and was rebuilt in the nearby Lightfoot Brewery cottages (Masham is positively marinated in beer).

There it minded its own business until closing in the late Nineties, lying sulkily unloved and rotting. It seems years of neglect can be almost as destructive as a Luftwaffe Dornier. Only the bench seating in the public bar, a stained-glass window shimmering with coopers hammering barrels, and a glass-encased polar bear were salvageable.

The bear was shot in Alaska in 1901 by John Cunliffe-Lister, 3rd Baron Masham, its bust donated to the pub by the Earl of Swinton to celebrate the wartime rebuild, but it was only during refurbishment in 2000 that its true stature was acknowledged. An expert engaged to clean it announced it was 'a Roland Ward, the Picasso of taxidermy' who had practised his craft in Harley Street.

Visitors are told the bear is actually standing upright in a corridor behind the public bar (and some of us swallow it). This room is as friendly a bar as you'd wish to relax in. The lounge bar and dining room next door fill quickly with a mix of daytripping ramblers and locals who know where to find the best lunch in town – and a welcoming fire on a wet January afternoon.

Silverside of beef or Yorkshire ham sandwich? Let's go for a door-stopping blue Wensleydale and beetroot (£4.95). Perfect. Specials include a robust wild boar burger (£10.95).

Had they met in the White Bear, Picasso and Old Peculier would have made natural companions: subtle yet intense, vibrant and simple. In other words, the bare necessities.

Alastair Gilmour, 12 January 2013

Wellgarth, Masham, North Yorkshire HG4 4EN (01765 689319); thewhitebearhotel.co.uk

North-East England

The Victoria Inn
Durham

When a barman's first job of the day is to fill a zinc bucket up with coal, you'd be right in thinking you're somewhere rare. The red-brick and sandstone Victoria Inn in Durham is indeed precious.

It has no external signage save for a small swinging board, while a couple of coach lamps and a row of pansy-profuse window boxes indicate 'pub'. But step inside and drink in 1899.

There's almost too much to adjust to.

Do your *Antiques Roadshow* aspirations soar at the sight of the back bar with its line-up of toby jugs, Victoria and Albert porcelain figurines and a caravan of loping elephants? Are 40 bottles of malt and 30 Irish whiskeys sparkling in the sunshine an utter delight? Do you long to rub your palm along the Cuban mahogany bar-top, die to press the keys of the Victorian brass till, or warm your backside over one of three black-leaded, tiled fireplaces?

First things first – choose one of the five cask ales, all from local microbreweries, then you can take time to examine photographs of the Durham Miners' Gala, 19th-century paintings of highland cattle, stags at bay and swooping eagles with added Victoriana shoehorned into what wall space is left.

The full-time beer is Big Lamp Bitter (3.9% ABV), an ale from Newcastle that shows off a fine balance of hop and malt, while a regular rotating selection includes the remarkable golden, softly fruity Jarrow Rivet Catcher (4.0% ABV) and Wylam Gold Tankard (4.0% ABV), a sharply flavoured, citrus-influenced beauty from Northumberland.

In the Victoria window seat, four domino-players click and clack away the afternoon, their concentration and passion convincing observers it should be an Olympic sport. The Grade II-listed Victoria is a three-roomed idyll with six letting rooms. Its Family Department and Sitting Room, with even more V&A memorabilia, speak of long-lost parlours. The timber flooring has been worn so smooth in parts it looks like linoleum, while wood panelling, shelving and mirrors blend with floral wallpaper in costume-drama proportions.

There is no television, no music and no food (unless crisps and pickled eggs are your thing) and the effect is such that it's said one customer ended up lingering over three pints – and he'd only come in to ask directions.

Landlord Michael Webster has been in The Victoria since 1974 and bought the pub outright in 1995 after owners Scottish & Newcastle had plans to alter it. He was determined to keep his pride and joy in Victorian attire.

'Pub companies pay fortunes to turn their places into something like this,' he says. 'This is as it's always been.'

It may operate in a time warp, but Olympian double-sixes and multiple awards are thoroughly today. The Victoria is weathering well; long may she reign.

Alastair Gilmour, 1 November 2014

86 Hallgarth Street, Durham DH1 3AS (0191 386 5269); victoriainn-durhamcity.co.uk

The Dun Cow
Sunderland

E verything that gives the Great British Pub its diversity
and contrast is condensed into the Dun Cow in
Sunderland. The handsomely refurbished Edwardian
building is a pageant of cornices, beading, fretwork and
dentil ornament. A small, gold-encrusted cow's head forms
the centrepiece of a stunning back bar.

Yet the company at the next table appears oblivious
to this extravagance as they compete to name as many
characters as possible from *The Beano*. 'I just love Gnasher,'
says one. Dennis the Menace's dog could demolish the
corbels and fillets above her head for breakfast, then go
back for egg-and-dart seconds. Someone else weighs in:
'Remember Pansy Potter?', though the ensuing anecdotes
suggest more a former colleague from the office than the
Strong Man's Daughter.

The Grade II-listed Dun Cow has benefited from a
£300,000 restoration programme driven by Sunderland
Music, Arts and Culture Trust. Sound investment, although
a touch more than the £2,000 that builder Thomas Pierce
Shaftoe received in 1902 for a year's sweat.

The pub's three storeys sit on a granite plinth topped by
two Dutch gables bearing brewing giant Robert Deuchar's
initials. A patinated copper-domed tower dominates one
corner. Its two clocks are stopped, though the one in the
bar is right so I managed to catch my scheduled train
home.

I've been lingering over Anarchy Blonde Star (4.1%
ABV), a crisply fresh light-bodied ale showing traces of

grapefruit and light biscuit malt which I've preferred to the Northumberland Brewery's Simcoe (4.1% ABV) as that one's a little too hop-heady for my present mood. I'll delay the rich coffee resuscitator Dark Star Espresso (4.2% ABV) until after lunch. And since the Dun Cow is a Camerons Brewery pub (operated under its Head of Steam brand), it would be impolite not to check on the legendary fruit and malt-loaf Strongarm (4.0% ABV).

The Head of Steam group promise is eight to ten cask and craft keg beers for bar hopping, served alongside inexpensive, home-cooked food and complemented by an occasional riff of live music. So the Dun Cow's 'tapas' menu has a hearty rhythm – slow-braised oxtail, Teesdale lamb casserole, Scottish moules marinière and a miscellany of burgers. But my money's on Doreen's black pudding with rosemary and garlic potatoes (£4.25).

The comic-loving characters have now taken note of their surroundings, discussing – in terms of 'magnificent' and 'remarkable' – decorative etching, the provenance of a mantelpiece, bevelled mirrors and stained-glass partitions guarding the neighbouring sitting room.

The Dun Cow has possibly never looked better in its 100-plus years – and it's not a bad place to enjoy a beano, either.

Alastair Gilmour, 28 March 2015

9 High Street West, Sunderland SR1 3HA (0191 567 2262); theheadofsteam.co.uk/pub?pub=11

The Sun Inn
Beamish Museum, County Durham

According to the newspaper I'm reading as a pint-chaser, there is 'alarming news from Salonica', the Pope's health is improving and Worth's corsets – 'unsurpassed for elegance' – are 12 shillings and sixpence a pair. It is an old newspaper.

It's dated 1913 and I'm surveying the day's events all the better to savour the historical ambience of The Sun Inn at Beamish Museum, County Durham.

The pub, like the rest of this award-winning open-air attraction, is time-warped just before the Great War. It sits among a clutch of buildings that constitute the Town, a short walk from the Pit Village, the Colliery, the Farm and the gentrified Pockerley Hall. Across the cobbled street, a Co-op and a motor dealer bring Victorian and Edwardian Britain alive with costumed staff escorting visitors down from trolley buses and trams.

The Sun Inn closes at 4pm – it has no regulars, but thousands of visitors – so I've got time to sup my way through three beers from the Stables Brewery, brewed (at risk of labouring historical references) only 40 chains distant. Beamish Hall (3.8% ABV), a traditional best bitter with toffee and green apple notes, is a belter of a starter. Silver Buckles (4.4% ABV) reveals grapefruit aromas then biscuit flavours, while an ascent to the dark and mysterious Bell Tower (5.0% ABV) finds a complex ale swirling with whiffs of chocolate and coffee. Food is a drove of pork pies inside a glass-covered cake stand. Thankfully fresh, not Edwardian.

In a previous life, The Sun was the Tiger Inn in Bishop Auckland before being rebuilt, stone by stone, on its present site in 1985. It is small, two-roomed, and utterly delightful. Porcelain jugs gleam, brass rails shine, and mirrors advertising John Walker & Son Kilmarnock Whisky shimmer, while a portrait of jockey Fred Archer peers across to 10st 10lb bricklayer and bare-knuckle boxer Tom Sawyer, who would fight anybody at any weight. Antlers and display cases of stuffed birds fill spaces alongside Jake's Bonny Mary, a whippet with nine handicaps to her credit in races as far apart as Newcastle, Carlisle and Cowdenbeath.

'Is it 1913 prices, then?' asks a hopeful customer. Starch-collared, waistcoated staff run a sweep on how many times the question will be posed. At the Co-op hardware store, brown-overalled workers play a similar game with 'fork handles'.

Coal fires tinkle in the Family Room and the Select Room, where you'd pay extra for discretion and upholstery, although the public bar's beautiful benches are surprisingly comfortable.

Bell Tower appeals as I scan the news: Sheffield Wednesday top Division One; Lord and Lady Knaresborough 'have arrived in London for the season'; Blayney's whisky is 24 shillings a gallon. At that price, put me down for 1913.

Alastair Gilmour, 28 February 2015

Beamish Museum, Beamish, County Durham DH9 0RG (0191 370 4000); beamish.org.uk

The Manor House Inn
Carterway Heads, Northumberland

The exchange rate at the Manor House Inn at Carterway Heads is dependent on what's in your carrier bag. A chalked sign in the doorway reads: 'Forage, shoot, grow or breed – have you got something we need?' So I estimate the pint and hot beef sandwich clutched by the chilled fisherman at the bar represents a couple of nicely weighted brown trout.

The 18th-century Manor House is the quintessential coaching inn, sitting on the undulating A68 at the head of the Derwent Reservoir, a noted watersports and wild fishing centre.

It's an inn in the old-fashioned sense – two-foot-thick sandstone walls coddle an absolute delight whether it's a meal, a few drinks, a short rest and recuperation exercise to admire the glorious North Pennines scenery, or a night or two's homely accommodation.

The public bar's enormous stone fireplace is an immediate focus but equally alluring is a large window onto the next-door cellar where the pub's functional innards are exposed to all and sundry. It's as if you've caught someone in a state of undress and you shouldn't really glimpse this room full of aluminium ale casks, plastic piping, junction boxes, pumpclips, bottles and boxes. It's a clever way of introducing a very tidy and well-organised operation – if the rest of the pub functions as efficiently as this appears to, everything else will be polished.

The fisherman's friend is a beer from North Shields named after a fairground ride. Cullercoats Shuggy Boat

Blonde (3.8% ABV) is lemon fruity and almost scented and one of a procession of ales flying the flag for northern interest that include the well-rounded Hadrian Border Farne Island Bitter (4.0% ABV) and Scottish Borders Game Bird (4.0% ABV), a delicately citrus-flavoured light amber ale. Between times, also expect short-hauled regulars from Consett Ale Works, Wylam and Allendale breweries.

Young's Old Gold (4.7% ABV) and Sharp's Doom Bar (4% ABV) appear on the visitors' guest list, while Morland Old Speckled Hen (4.5% ABV) is the house beer, but brewed 200 miles away in Suffolk, it's a curious choice for a pub fiercely high on regionality.

A full dining room on a weekday lunchtime suggests the food is worth travelling for – visitors regularly drive the 30 minutes from Newcastle or Durham. Ingredients such as Northumbrian belly pork, pigeon breast, venison and pheasant are drizzled in local provenance and it may well be that one of the bartered fish is about to grace my dish of whole roast trout, chorizo, creamy white wine sauce and seasonal vegetables (£14).

Back in the allotment I search for some vegetables to convert into Manor House Inn beer. An armful of beetroot, a string of onions, an arsenal of leeks; what to choose? One potato, two potato, three potato, four ...

Alastair Gilmour, 10 May 2014

Carterway Heads, Northumberland DH8 9LX (01207 255268); themanorhouseinn.com

The Dipton Mill Inn
Hexham, Northumberland

Draw the definitive English country pub and it would
look like the Dipton Mill Inn, near Hexham in
Northumberland. Describe a coaching inn interior and it
would be low-ceilinged and solid-beamed with five ales on
the bar and a tinkling log fire – much like the Dipton Mill
Inn.

Now specify the perfect landlord. The publican would be
rotund and bearded. He'd be a jolly soul, a slight eccentric
who chuckles at his own jokes, draping tales in wit and
whimsy. Regular customers have heard the stories before, but
that's half the fun. You couldn't make Geoff Brooker up.*

The Dipton Mill Inn is the quintessential English
country pub: sitting by a stream in the middle of nowhere,
skirted by woodland crisscrossed by rambling trails, and
surrounded by agricultural acres.

A mill race loops around the building – a 17th-century
farmhouse – and its suntrap of a beer garden. Licensee
records show it has been a pub since 1820. Beer is
exclusively from the landlord's Hexhamshire microbrewery,
a couple of miles away.

On the bar are Devil's Water (4.1% ABV), a fruity,
copper-hued best bitter; award-winning Shire Bitter (3.8%
ABV), an easy drinker with a delicious hop and fruit
balance; plus Devil's Elbow (3.6% ABV) and Whapweasel
(4.8% ABV). Blackhall English Stout (4.0% ABV) has
proved so popular it has eased Guinness from the counter.
Brooker also brews Old Humbug (5.5% ABV), a winter ale
he's considered stocking year round.

However, an outlying pub couldn't survive on liquid alone, and the lunchtime chalkboard that includes chicken breast in sherry sauce, lambs' liver and sausages and three-cheese ploughman's accounts for 40% of trade. Mince and dumplings and steak and kidney pie are bestsellers, received wisdom being that these days people rarely cook such staples for themselves.

More importantly, everything is home-made by the landlord's wife (who also compiles the pub's quiz questions).

Forty-odd years ago, an episode of *The Likely Lads* was filmed outside – a reshot and reshot sequence with Bob and Terry cycling up and down and using the phone box. It's not that nothing ever happens here, but people still talk about it.

Hexhamshire Brewery beer mats scattered around the pub feature its logo, a Thomas Bewick 18th-century woodcut depicting two men in brimmed hats and breeches with a wooden barrel suspended between them. It was quite a while before an elderly visitor pointed out that they weren't lugging beer, as folks had naturally thought.

'It's a reference to the local leather tanning industry,' she said. 'It's urine.' People still talk about it.

Alastair Gilmour, 1 June 2013

---

* Sadly, Geoff Brooker died in January 2015, but the pub, run by his wife and son Mark, lives on and is thankfully unchanged.

Dipton Mill Inn, Dipton Mill Road, Hexham, Northumberland NE46 1YA (01434 606577); diptonmill.co.uk

The Lion & Lamb
Horsley, Northumberland

The Lion & Lamb was originally built as a farmhouse in 1718, using stones from nearby Hadrian's Wall. It was converted into a coaching inn soon afterwards, and is now a pretty, white-painted pub in the centre of the small Northumberland village of Horsley. Inside, the stone walls are exposed and, in the main bar, the floor is flagstoned, yet the atmosphere is warm and friendly.

The staff are friendly, too, although the barman looks as if he has just found out that he's been disinherited by his multi-millionaire parents. The two waitresses are clearly enjoying their work and Geordie banter passes easily between them. The manager is very proud of his traditional borderland boozer. After chatting for ten minutes, he gives us a voucher for 10% off the bill on future visits.

There are exposed beams and rustic wooden tables and chairs in the bar and restaurant, and leather armchairs in the room overlooking the magnificent distant views of the Tyne Valley. In summer, the French doors open onto a patio and beer garden that face south and make the most of the vista from the pub's elevated position.

The schoolroom-like restaurant has a wooden floor, brass ornaments and a scattering of agricultural implements. On the starters menu are crab and prawn tian (served with Bloody Mary jelly and guacamole purée) and duck and black pudding hash. I opt for venison terrine, which comes with home-made beetroot and apple chutney and toast.

For the main course I am tempted by the locally made Northumberland sausage (only £8.95) and the pavé rump of beef with parsnip purée and salt-baked new potatoes. Instead I choose smoked haddock on a cheese, leek and bacon mash with whole-grain mustard sauce and a poached egg (£12.50). The food is excellent and good value, and the beers are good, too. They are fairly local, with the excellent Wylam brewery and Big Lamp brewery at Newburn featuring. A pint of Black Sheep bitter is too difficult to resist, however, and it doesn't disappoint.

Also on offer is a tapas menu (three for £9.95) and a pasta menu. On the chalkboard dessert menu, the summer fruit pudding sounds good, but the delightfully named toffee apple meltdown has to be tried. The Lion & Lamb has rooms that can be booked for functions and special events. It's all go here – Wednesday night is steak night: two steaks and a bottle of wine for £25, and Sunday night is quiz night; included in the £2 entry is a pie and pea supper.

The villages along the Tyne Valley are all interesting and, of course, Hadrian's Wall is well worth a visit. If you travel this way, you really ought to drop in at the Lion & Lamb. It's not so grim up north.

Ed Jowsey, 31 January 2015

Horsley, Newcastle upon Tyne, Northumberland NE15 0NS (01661 852952); lionlamb-horsley.co.uk

The Centurion
Newcastle upon Tyne

Tetchy and saddle-sore, and a little down in the mouth at being daughterless again after dropping mine off at her mother's cottage in Northumberland ('They don't mess about with the grass up here, do they?') for two weeks, I found myself changing trains in one of the country's finest stations – a station, by purest coincidence, that's home to one of the country's finest bars. An invisible filament – let's call it the 'beer bungee' – drew me across the threshold. I could always get the 13.52, I thought.

The Centurion was initially Grand Central Station's waiting room – designed, like the station and much of the town around it, by architect John Dobson. It was sumptuously redecorated and rebranded as a 'refreshment room' in the 1890s. Later, with that cack-handed indifference to historical interiors that our country's institutions so often exhibit, the British Transport Police took it over, daubing its tiled walls with red paint and chopping up the space into holding cells. It's since been restored beautifully – save for a large and distinctly iffy landscape painting – and has served as a 'café bar', albeit one pubby enough to qualify for inclusion in the P to P corpus, I hope you'll agree, since 2000.

The space is high, wide and handsome – a great neoclassical interior in the vein of the assembly rooms of York, Cheltenham and Bath, but also nodding, in its opulent, eclectic decor (ceramics by Burmantofts of Leeds, if you're interested), to the gin palaces of its own time. A bar at one end dispenses spirits, wines and beers including the obligatory Newcastle Brown Ale (pint bottle, half-pint glass).

A little row of handpumps to one side promised unfamiliar (to me) but patently local and artisanal beers; but I plumped for a thirst-quenching, sappy Estrella – '... in a thin glass', in homage to *Get Carter.*

A range of food options is mostly consumed in a little brasserie-ish annexe sitting on the platform, but in the main bar you can get Whitby scampi, North Sea cod and chips and various bready iterations including 'panninis' (sic) and a 'posh fish finger sandwich'.

One cannot live by fine Victorian architecture, cask-conditioned ales and high-quality bar snacks alone, however. It's the people that make the place. Even on this hungover Sunday lunchtime, the Centurion rang with laughter and 'bantz': the lads grey-eyed and bullet-headed, half an eye cocked towards the sport (they have sport, but it's not intrusive); the lassies profound of cleavage, richly anointed in slap, teetering on their cork wedges; all hoisting their glasses high like the Eagle of the Ninth, trading jokes and stories in their distinctive lowing voices, filling the space with a joyful hullabaloo.

Keith Miller, 22 August 2015

Grand Central Station, Neville Street, Newcastle upon Tyne NE1 5DG (0191 261 6611); centurion-newcastle.com

The Bridge Hotel
Newcastle upon Tyne

The view from the Bridge Hotel in Newcastle is a lesson in the city's history. Across the cobbled square in front of the 1901-vintage pub sits the Castle Keep, constructed in 1080 by Maurice the Engineer (also responsible for Dover Castle); to one side is Robert Stephenson's double-deck High Level Bridge (1849) and squatting on the other is the 1812, Grade I-listed, Greek revival Moot Hall.

The Bridge is even reputed to have a section of Roman pavement in its cellar – and how many beer gardens employ a near 1,000-year-old city wall as an elbow-rest?

Antiquity thrives in this corner of Newcastle, but the popular pub is not entirely preserved in alcohol, and has been altered significantly to suit modern demands, thankfully with a dollop of architectural sympathy. Its polished wooden panelling, unfussy chandeliers, sparkling engraved mirrors and original back bar might tug a forelock to yesteryear, but like many city pubs, it has to cater for a wide range of clientele, drawn by the quality of its beer, the lunchtime menu and the buzz that animates evenings.

Interior details can be studied on quieter occasions, such as the original architects' elevations framed on one wall. The drawings emphasise what a handsome chap the building is too. Extensive bookshelves are open for exploration and, judging by the dog-eared nature of some of the contents, it's a regular pastime. Pleasures for riffling through include two volumes of the *Concise Home Doctor, The Spy Who Came In From The Cold*, and *Who's Who 1973*.

The menu includes the gastronomic combination defining that particular era – gammon steak, chips, fried egg and pineapple relish (£6.50) – and also Cumberland sausage curl and creamy mash with onion and ale gravy (£6.95), plus a selection of sandwiches (£4.50).

However, it's beer that the Bridge is renowned for – eleven real ales and craft keg beers, and much of it local. Hadrian Border High Level Bitter (4% ABV), a solidly malty and full-on Scottish-style ale, is brewed little more than two miles away. Anarchy Blonde Star (4.1%), from a dozen miles north, has citrus hops to the fore; Black Sheep Golden Sheep (4.7%) is as refreshing, straightforward and reliable as beer comes, as is Deuchars IPA (3.8%). Unpasteurised Budweiser Budvar Yeast Beer (5%) – once a visitor, now in residency – is a remarkable example of Czech brewing heritage.

The Bridge and traditional music enjoy a long association. The pub has played host to folk band the High Level Ranters (who influenced fiddler and Northumbrian smallpipes wizz Kathryn Tickell), the Seventies folk-rock group Lindisfarne and even superstar Sting. So what if its *Who's Who* is a little dated? This is a pub that knows what's what.

Alastair Gilmour, 11 May 2013

Castle Garth, Newcastle upon Tyne NE1 1RQ (0191 232 6400); sjf.co.uk/our-pubs/bridge-hotel

The Bridge Tavern
Newcastle upon Tyne

First-time visitors to Newcastle quayside would be forgiven for thinking one of its pubs had two names. A swinging sign announces The Bridge Tavern; yet the words Newcastle Arms stand proud on its sandstone fascia.

A previously neglected pub and nightspot was gutted and restyled in 2013, but the relief lettering was retained as it would have been 'architectural vandalism' to hack it off. Such sensitivity in pub refurbishment is exceptional but it's an appropriate introduction to what lies inside.

The Bridge interior owes much to the school of exposed innards, with ducting and services extending across the ceiling. Areas of brickwork, joists, joints and cast concrete suggest a utilitarian idea of beauty. It hunkers so neatly under the stanchions of the Tyne Bridge that the roof terrace is sheltered from all but the worst of the North East climate by its bare green belly.

Back in the main bar, a random sampling of the offbeat library donated by a local jazz café owner reveals a copy of *American Combat Planes, The Theory and Practice of Heat Engines* and the *Radiation Cookery Book*, which includes a recipe for Free Kirk pudding, an austere mix of flour, currants and breadcrumbs.

The Bridge has driven a Newcastle brewpub wave that's creating more interest in beer styles and niche production than at any time in living memory. A microbrewery and bar-eatery, it's aimed squarely at the drinker and diner seeking style and sophistication wrapped in traditional familiarity.

I'm greeted by a slowly dissipating aroma of malted barley from an early-morning brew. Today's 360-pint batch of Tavernales, produced in the beautiful stainless-steel and copper vessels, looking like the support act to an international space programme, will be different from yesterday's – and tomorrow's. However, the more popular recipes are reintroduced, such as Chachapoya (3.8% ABV), an amber-hued aromatic ale with overtones of autumnal fruit, and American Broon (4.7% ABV), a sweetish, malty, transatlantic version of Newcastle Brown Ale (now brewed in Tadcaster). They're supplemented by a regular supply of local Wylam Brewery ales, including the sensationally bittersweet Jakehead IPA (6.3% ABV), and significant guests in cask and keg from the likes of Dark Star, Redemption and Camden Town breweries.

The menu focuses on seasonal comfort food 'with a local twist', led by meat and fish sharing planks (£11.95).

Free Kirk pudding has yet to appear.

Alastair Gilmour, 17 October 2015

7 Akenside Hill, Newcastle upon Tyne NE1 3UF (0191 261 9966); thebridgetavern.com

The Free Trade Inn
Newcastle upon Tyne

I t's open to question whether Newcastle's Free Trade Inn was the inspiration for a catchy Tyneside song. But one thing's for sure, the chorus paints an accurate picture.

'Oh the sunsets bonny lad/ Oh the sunsets bonny lad/ There's a bobby dazzlin' sunset every day.'

The view of the River Tyne from the pub includes much that Newcastle has to be proud of – its iconic bridges, Baltic Centre for Contemporary Art and the Sage Centre for Music form an industrial and culture-rich backdrop to a resurgent city.

The Free Trade Inn's vantage point is above the Ouseburn Valley, sitting to the east of the city centre, and a position that allows it to lord over what could be termed Newcastle's artists' quarter. Several attempts by developers to forest the area with high-rise apartments have been howled down by customers who don't see why their panorama should be compromised.

The Free Trade Inn has basked in an independent spirit for more than 30 years, which is a huge part of its appeal. The deliberately 'basic' pub attracts a wide ranging clientele, from musicians and craftspeople in neighbouring collectives, to office workers who relish the escape from Newcastle's party city reputation.

Its current status as Tyneside's Pub of the Year is ever more reason to visit, with newcomers marvelling at its nicotine-inspired colour scheme.

It's almost impossible to keep up with the range of beers – ten hand-pulls sit happily alongside long-hauled Brooklyn lager and Budweiser Budvar, plus a wide selection of ciders. One popular beer festival featured several Italian craft brews, some of them astonishing in flavour and style, like the golden Toccalmatto Grooving Hop (4.5% ABV). In the main, however, beers are sourced locally and there are now so many microbreweries within cask-commuting distance, everybody gets a look-in sooner or later.

Tyne Bank and Out There breweries are within aroma-shot, with the former's Peloton Pale Ale (3.7% ABV) possibly more popular among regulars than Craig David, the pub's resident cat. But Mordue Workie Ticket (4.5% ABV), a well-balanced bitter, is about as permanent as a beer gets here.

Gateshead-born music maker Alex Glasgow wrote 'The Sunsets, Bonny Lad' and performed it with the Northern Sinfonia, although sadly it doesn't feature on the jukebox alongside Talking Heads and Tom Waits.

The Free Trade Inn could never be described as 'foodie' but pies from the Amble Butcher and sandwiches from the renowned Dene's Deli set the snack bar as high as the ale offering.

Taken with a pint of unfiltered Anarchy Rough Justice (4.5% ABV) in one of two well-appointed beer gardens, they elevate an already dazzlin' experience.

Alastair Gilmour, 27 July 2013

St Lawrence Road, Ouseburn, Newcastle upon Tyne NE6 1AP
(0191 265 5764); facebook.com/TheFreeTradeInn

St Mary's Inn
Stannington, Northumberland

A little cairn of smouldering logs in a wood-burning stove can sharpen an appetite like nothing else. A crystal-clear lunchtime ale with one eye on next-door's beer-battered cod sandwich certainly comes close – as do the vanilla and tobacco aromas from a twelve-year-old malt, one of 46 seducing me at St Mary's Inn in Stannington, Northumberland.

The resinous aroma radiates from two stoves and a large fireplace that cheer three snug bars in this medley of pub, restaurant and accommodation, knitted together in a con-verted hospital administration building dating from 1910.

Elegantly tall windows flank the arched main door, while a red-brick frontage trimmed with yellow bandings, then topped by a handsome clock tower, lend the air of a film set. A framed text on the wall sets out the building's history. George Thomas Hine was, from 1897, consulting architect to the Commissioners of Lunacy. Full marks to the pub owners for presenting social history in warts-and-all frankness. In the meantime, JCBs munch away at the former ward blocks to create a 136-acre, des-res, 'brand-new community'.

At the bar, a specially developed St Mary's Ale (4% ABV) and zesty, citrus Collingwood (4.1% ABV) come from Wylam, the progressive Northumberland brewery, both bolstered by Mordue Radgie Gadgie (4.8% ABV), a delightful example of a northern premium bitter. Craft keg beers are also from Northumberland brewery Allendale, and Anarchy, less than a mile away.

The menu promises honest British classics, wringing as many local references as possible from the likes of braised lamb mince with dumplings and rare breed pork sausage and mash – and who could resist that regional delicacy, ham and pease-pudding stottie?

Accompanying my St Mary's Ale at a solid, unshakeable table (no need to fold a steadying beer mat) is a 1989 copy of *Northern Goalfields*, plucked from the shelves behind me. This history of the Northern League, the world's second-oldest football competition, is told through a century of Blyth Spartans, Billingham Synthonia and Tow Law Town. There's also a set of Wainwright Lakeland guides, but four Stephen Fry novels is four too many for my liking.

A scout around the pub uncovers a couple of Norman Cornish paintings. Chronicler of pitmen, pubs, street life and washdays, Cornish captured honest workers and double-crossing domino players with wit and vigour. I pay particular attention to the two men pictured at a bar with a whippet on a lead – I've got a print of it at home. Another sip of St Mary's Ale suppresses a 'one-of-these-days' sigh.

Alastair Gilmour, 14 February 2015

St Mary's Lane, St Mary's Park, Stannington, Morpeth, Northumberland NE61 6BL (01670 293293); stmarysinn.co.uk

The Jolly Fisherman
Craster, Northumberland

Two male eider ducks are fighting as their female prize preens nonchalantly. Beyond them, the waves are crashing on the rocks and up the sides of the harbour walls. We have a pint of Mordue Workie Ticket in our hands and are somewhat smugly basking in what must be one of the most perfectly positioned beer gardens in England, at The Jolly Fisherman in lovely Craster.

The gate next to us leads on to St Oswald's Way, otherwise known as the Northumberland Coast Path; those trudging along it from Hadrian's Wall to the south or Holy Island to the north cross directly into the grounds of 'The Jolly'. It must be a welcome relief to be told that 'muddy boots and dogs [are] welcome'.

The view to the other side of the beer garden is of the majestic ruin of Dunstanburgh Castle just a mile and a half away. On this clear day, its outline resembles a pair of jagged scissors cutting into blue silk. Further beyond is the dune-backed beach at Embleton Bay.

The Jolly Fisherman has been a feature of this fishing village since 1847, but a refurbishment this year made more of its stunning coastal location, creating spectacular vistas through bigger restaurant windows as well as an outdoor terrace. There are open fires for stormy days, stone-flagged floors, low-beamed ceilings, battered leather sofas – but nothing is twee or ostentatious: think Farrow & Ball colours and muted herringbone upholstery. We adored this pub – in all its tattiness – on a visit on a rainy day last September, when a cosy snug and roaring fire was blissful, but really, we love this shinier mantle even more.

Owned by David Whitehead, a former professional rugby player, the menu embraces the best of the Northumberland larder, and the Jolly is rightly proud of its crab sandwiches, crab soup and Craster kipper mousse.

As well as the Workie Ticket, from Mordue's nearby-ish Wallsend brewery, regular cask beers include Black Sheep, from Yorkshire, and Timothy Taylor Landlord. The monthly guest ale was Tetley's Gold on our visit, but it could be Golden Sheep, or WharfeBank Brewery's Celtic Red. A wine list comprises three whites, three reds and a California zinfandel rosé.

With the sign for the ladies' tagged 'fishwives' and the pictures on the wall depicting the fine art of herring-gutting being practised by beefy women in voluminous skirts, it would be remiss of any but the fish-loathing visitor to leave Craster without a packet of kippers. And so, after quenching our drouth, we hop across the road to L. Robson & Sons, with its shop among the sheds where the village's kippers are smoked. Thus armed, we hit the coastal path again, feeling most jolly.

Audrey Gillan, 6 July 2013

Haven Hill, Craster, Northumberland NE66 3TR (01665 576461); thejollyfishermancraster.co.uk

The Red Lion Inn
Milfield, Northumberland

E xactly 500 years ago on Monday, Henry VIII's army marched to Northumberland to engage with James IV, King of Scots and his force of 35,000 men. The English, under the command of Thomas Howard, Earl of Surrey, expected battle to commence on a flat plain sheltered by the Cheviot Hills – 'a goodly and large cornfield called Milfield' – but were dismayed to discover the Scots had assembled on a hill at nearby Flodden.

Remarkably, the cornfield is still there, so from the beer garden of Milfield's Red Lion Inn, it's not difficult to imagine the historic scene. Five centuries ago, soldiers would have been studying battle plans on this very spot – and here are we, discussing Black Sheep Best Bitter while picking through a menu of honey-roast pork belly and pan-fried salmon fillet with garlic king prawns.

Milfield – population 200 – sits midway between Edinburgh and Newcastle and inevitably the stone-built Red Lion Inn developed from its mid-18th-century origins into a stopoff for mail coaches. Now fishermen, golfers, shooting parties and tourists benefit from Claire and Iain Burn's simple innkeeping principles: well-kept ale, wholesome food, efficient service and a bed for the night.

A huge load-bearing beam across the pub's main room doubles as a chalkboard for local produce. It also reads like the itinerary for a Border Reivers' raiding party. Norham, Ford and Doddington villages are not only within cannon-shot; their respective butchery, bakery and dairy products are justifiably highly regarded.

The Red Lion is divided neatly into three dining areas of descending size and increasing intimacy and a separate, simply furnished public bar. Here the counter is well worn, nicked and kicked which, with its elbow-smoothed areas along the top, expresses the scars of hospitality.

Alongside the consistent Black Sheep (3.8% ABV), beers include Signal Main Line IPA (3.6%), a citrus-led refresher from North Yorkshire, and the nicely balanced Allendale 1513 (3.8%), brewed near Northumberland's boundary with Cumbria.

During conversation – usually farming talk, the gliding club or the leek show – it emerges that Red Lion regulars are known by their occupations or habits. The Byreman gets a mention, as does Lawnmower Salesman. Presently someone asks: 'Brown Ale Man been in?'

On 9 September 1513, the wily Earl of Surrey outmanoeuvred the Scots and the ferocious Battle of Flodden commenced at 4pm, leaving 14,000 men dead – including James himself.

In today's Red Lion there's little chance of being caught up in cross-border warfare. Somebody's more likely to sell you a lawnmower.

Alastair Gilmour, 7 September 2013

Main Road, Milfield, Wooler, Northumberland NE71 6JD (01688 216224); redlionmilfield.co.uk

Scotland

The Oxford Bar
Edinburgh

Along a cobbled street in Edinburgh's glorious New Town sits an incongruous building that looks for all the world like it belongs in a small market town or halfway up a mountain in Wales, not in the centre of the Scottish Enlightenment.

It is painted white, with two small etched windows and a simple black door. The sign hanging above it says The 'Oxford' Bar, the inverted commas a puzzle to many.

This sign draws in not just Edinburgh drinkers but crime fiction fans keen to sup a pint in Detective Inspector John Rebus's favourite bar. For the hard-nosed protagonist of Ian Rankin's novels is wont to seek solace in the 'tap room' or back snug of this aged establishment.

Given its dark wood bar, brass pumps and step-back-in-time decor, it is not hard to see why Rankin would choose this as the drinking den of his fictional creation. Writing about the place affectionately known as the Ox, Rankin has said: 'The Oxford Bar is great because it's like a private members' club. The first time you go in you're a stranger; the second time they know what you drink and they're pulling the pint before you get to the bar. It's very small and homely, with just two rooms; the back room has church pews for chairs. It has a traditional Edinburgh atmosphere. It hasn't changed in a hundred years or so.'

He's not wrong. In the snug, the pale blue walls may have had a fresh lick, but the lino is worn, the leather on the church-style benches beaten thin with the pressure of many a bottom, the light dancing through the windows in summer, the fire flickering in the hearth in winter. Among the pictures portraying Edinburgh throughout the ages is a nostalgic photo of the Ox from many decades ago – it still looks very much the same.

The tap room bears little totems of the pub's literary sensibility: a portrait of Robert Burns; a bookshelf lined with dictionaries and beer, film and music guides. There's an old-school 'custodian' – or bobby's – helmet, more Dixon of Dock Green than Rebus of St Leonards' Nick.

On his visits, Rankin is a fan of Deuchars IPA, made a few miles away at the city's last remaining brewery, Caledonian, a place that fills Edinburgh's air with heady hops – it's a pale golden session ale, but it leaves us wondering why the author finds it so special. But the pumps also offer up Bellhaven 80 Shilling; deep, malty Lia Fail from Inveralmond Brewery; and sweet yet citrusy Harviestoun Bitter and Twisted.

Don't come to the Ox expecting to find John Rebus or, indeed, Ian Rankin. Come to find a place that transports you through time, with punters who'll no doubt make you feel like an auld, auld friend.

Audrey Gillan, 3 October 2015

8 Young Street, Edinburgh EH2 4JB (0131 539 7119); oxfordbar.co.uk

The Bridge Inn
Ratho, Midlothian

Do we reach a stage in life that compels us to wave a lot? Clutching my pint outside The Bridge Inn at Ratho, in Midlothian, I'm beginning to wonder if, for me, the moment is nigh.

A narrowboat slips along the adjacent Union Canal. I wave. Dog walkers follow the towpath opposite. I wave. Cyclists whirr past. Wave. Red-faced joggers, power-walkers; up goes the hand. The sequence of greetings is entertainment in itself, but I hope the gestures are taken as me being at ease on a sunny terrace outside a beautiful pub rather than as a draining of faculties.

The Bridge Inn, eight miles west of Edinburgh city centre, is one of Scotland's most decorated pubs, gathering plaudits and awards for Best Food Pub, Dog Friendliest Pub, and Pub of the Year over the past few years. And it deserves every one.

The pub's location is as magnificent as it is practical. Ratho is a delightful village minutes from Edinburgh Airport, and the pub owners' walled garden sitting beyond a clutch of bonny canalside cottages renders the kitchen seasonally self-sufficient.

Its beer is fiercely Scottish – from Fyne Ales, Knops, Alechemy, Arran and Orkney breweries – and the bar food is highlighted by cullen skink, a classic creamy, smoked haddock, potato and leek soup. (A top-notch bistro is part of the set-up, but we've waived that to choose between a bargeman's sandwich – Isle of Mull cheddar and homemade pickle – and beetroot hummus, olives and peashoots, chased by a 'paddle' selection of indigenous ales.) The pub's ageless barge offers weekend dining trips, with one regular excursion ferrying rugby fans to matches at Murrayfield.

But there is a slight chill coming off the water and, nipping indoors for an alternative to the full-bodied, fruity Skye Blaven (5%), I'm encouraged to take my choice (Cairngorm Black Gold, 4.4%) into a small lounge because 'there's a wee fire on in there, so it's nice and comfy'. Being more of a bar habitué, I'm content to be part of the mismatched fittings, framed local scenes, solid furniture and undulations of upholstery.

I feel almost as comfortable as the chap beside me with his spread-out newspaper, pint glass acting like a magnifier, flat cap hanging on his chair. An acquaintance crosses the car park and semaphores the universal 'ready for another' signal; that unmistakable wiggly hand action and raised eyebrow. Cap man nods and tilts his chestnut-coloured Knops Musselburgh Broke (4.5%) towards his mate. It would appear that good things come in waves.

Alastair Gilmour, 4 July 2015

27 Baird Road, Ratho, Midlothian EH28 8RA (0131 333 1320); bridgeinn.com

The Grill
Aberdeen

'I 'll have a glass of whisky,' said the chap next to me, and the smartly attired barman (white shirt, black trousers) opened a glass case behind him and pulled out a bottle.

As one does, while standing at the bar counter, I was tuning in and out of the conversations around me: office gossip and the general chaff of pub talk. I took a sip of American Pale Ale from Windswept, a brewery whose name suggested wild Scottish shores. The golden beer burst with citrus and bittersweet notes and went down smoothly.

A dram was poured and handed over. 'That'll be £35.40.' My reverie was interrupted and I turned to ask if he had really just paid that much for a dram. He nodded and told me it was a 1938 Speyside from a long-closed distillery. 'Worth every penny.'

We talked more.

My new acquaintance was on leave from the rigs and let it be known he was a bit of a whisky connoisseur. He offered me a sniff of the glass and I noted a mellowed-out ghost of sherry and sweetness – but whether it was worth it I didn't know.

Chastened by my ignorance, I lifted a glass in salute and went and sat down at a table and took in my surroundings.

Even though its name suggests otherwise, The Grill doesn't do food, unless you count meat pies. However, this solid-looking boozer slotted into a granite-faced terrace on Aberdeen's Union Street was once an eating place. In 1926 it changed tack and became a pub, and as well as its impeccable cask beers (usually five), incredible whisky selection and lively clientele, it also retains many of its original fixtures and fittings.

I took in the imposing ceiling with its patterned plasterwork, the mahogany-panelled walls and the hand-carved gantry above the bar. This was being propped up by a wide variety of after-work drinkers, chatting amiably.

The Grill didn't always provide this level of sociability: when it first opened, women were banned. This lasted until 1975, though it would take another 23 years before a ladies' loo was built.

I popped up to get a refill and, sitting down, noticed the elderly gent on the next table. He was getting ready to go. He adjusted his hat and scarf, took a look at his polished brogues and turned for the door, but not before saying his farewells to the bar staff and a group of drinkers in the corner.

I got the feeling he had been coming to The Grill for a long time; he looked at home. Off he went into the night and I knew he would be back tomorrow and the day after.

I would, too, if I lived in Aberdeen: The Grill is that kind of pub, a place where both conversation and contemplation can be enjoyed in equal measures.

Adrian Tierney-Jones, 8 August 2015

213 Union Street, Aberdeen AB11 6BA (01224 573530); thegrillaberdeen.co.uk

The Applecross Inn
Applecross, Wester Ross

The rocky beach beside the Applecross Inn might qualify it as the quietest watering hole in the British Isles. From our shoreside table we gaze across the slate-coloured sea toward the majestic Cuillins of Skye, receding in layers of dark, hard granite, then soft pewter and, eventually, hazy blue. A solitary kayak skims past a whitewashed cottage on the far shore and a cyclist, conspicuous in a riot of Lycra, dismounts at the waterside. Our hushed reverence for the serene grandeur is quickly destroyed by my excitable young niece Betty: 'What does "tranquil" mean?' She is not conducive to otter spotting.

The journey here is as sublime as the destination. It's a rollercoaster ride over the Bealach na Bà, which, at 2,053 feet, is the highest mountain pass in Britain. Its one-in-five gradients and white-knuckle hairpins would test the stiff upper lip of Richard Hannay of *Thirty-Nine Steps* fame. On a clear day the views of Raasay and beyond are breathtaking.

On arrival you might feel in need of a stiff one from the extensive range of malt whiskies behind the bar. A stuffed otter stands to attention in a glass case above the wood-burning stove, and the walls are strewn with stag and dog pictures. Large windows offer views of the pub's enormous sustainable larder, Applecross Bay itself.

The aptly named Judith Fish, who hails from Yorkshire and has owned the pub since 1989, explains how the scallops are hand-dived, the prawns trapped in traditional creels and the fish line-caught whenever possible. An ex-school dinner lady, Judith now employs the services of local chef Robert Macrae, who trained under the Roux brothers in London.

We order plump langoustines with garlic butter and crusty bread. They're as sweet and fresh as the sea air. Our crab arrives, dressed to the nines, with Torridon smoked salmon on the side. The salmon can be ordered as a snack, either regular cold-smoked or flaked hot-smoked. In season, whole deer are brought here from the Applecross estate and butchered in situ by Macrae, a master butcher, who makes casseroles and burgers, and loin of venison for favoured customers.

On our visit, draft ales include dry, hoppy Young Pretender (4%) and thirst-quenching Hebridean Gold (4.3%), both from the Isle of Skye Brewery, and malty, bittersweet An Teallach Ale (4.2%), made in the classic Scottish '80 shilling' style on the shores of Little Loch Broom. Bottled beers include straw-coloured Corncrake Ale (4.1%) from the Orkneys, Black Isle Organic Porter (4.6%) and deep red Loch Ness (4.4%) made with organic porridge oats.

There are seven en suite bedrooms, which, judging by visitors' comments, seem to encourage marriage proposals. Must be the oysters.

Jonathan Goodall, 13 December 2014

Applecross, Wester Ross, IV54 8LR (01520 744262); applecross.uk.com/inn

Drygate
Glasgow

I had been daundering among the dead, crossing over the 'Bridge of Sighs' and climbing up into Glasgow's Necropolis, a cluster of tombs and tributes to the merchants who built what was once the second city of the Empire. Now I was on the way back downhill, on the lookout for an ancient artesian spring known as the Ladywell, whose waters had once refreshed the Romans – and nowadays nourish the Tennent Caledonian brewery at Wellgate.

But what I hadn't anticipated was stumbling on a tiny new brewery that has just now popped up by the behemoth's side: Drygate Brewing Co, which (I later discovered) is described by marketeers as the UK's first '"experiential" craft brewery'. Beneath the seven-toothed roof of an old box factory (which has also inspired Drygate's logo) sits a brewery, restaurant, beer hall, events space, sun terrace and bottle shop. On a board at the gate are chalked the words, 'Welcome to Drygate: great beer and great beards'. This proved to be true on both counts.

This is the oldest area of Glasgow, but the beards signified that it may be on the way to becoming one of the trendiest. Inside, the main restaurant and bar area is all mild steel, cast concrete, solid wood and shiny light fittings. But what is truly glorious is the polished patinated copper of the barback and counter. It is here that you can lurk, working your way along the taps, tasting in thirds, halves or pints.

There are 24 different beers on tap here, with three of Drygate's own at its core: Bearface Lager (4.4% ABV),

Outaspace Apple Ale (4.7%) and Gladeye IPA (5.5%). It was a hot day on my serendipitous visit so the Apple Ale was just the ticket – fresh, easy and moreish, it apparently sells by the clichéd barrel-load when the sun is out. The Bearface was almost lemony; the Gladeye had a hint of pineapple interwoven with its hoppiness. But it was the special Rin Stout (conjured up by young brewer Jake Griffin) that supplied me with my second surprise of the day – there's chocolate and coffee in here and it's £3 for just one-third of a pint (it's 8.8%).

But what makes Drygate different, the thing that puts the experience in 'experiential', is the floor-to-ceiling picture window that affords a view on to the brewkit. Grab a table looking right into the 24-hectolitre plant and taste a flight of the beer you are watching being brewed before you. Or step inside and learn to brew your own under tutelage – here the motto is: 'Brewed Fearlessly: Achieve the Exceptional'.

There's a mesh-clad shop with beer bottles as walls, offering more than 200 different bottled beers to take away. So you can come and sup at Drygate's well then stagger off home with a few for later. But come early. The hipsters may claim outright ownership towards the wee small hours.

Audrey Gillan, 26 July 2014

85 Drygate, Glasgow G4 0UT (0141 212 8810); drygate.com

The West Kirk
Ayr

Traditionally, the pub is the place you visit after church. At this elegantly vaulted establishment, however, the church (well, former church) is the pub.

What's more, the West Kirk retains more than a few of its ecclesiastical features. It has a raised wooden pulpit, a first-floor balcony for worshipper overspill, plus a soaring, pointy-spired frontage that clearly signposts the way to heaven. Not to mention a massive suspended light fitting that hovers over the congregation of quaffers like an outsized flying saucer.

There are, however, certain elements that you don't get in the average apse. Like the wall-to-wall carpet, and the 50-yard bar, with outlets that dispense beer rather than holy wine. And booth seating, as well as open-plan tables out in the middle of the room, where the Reverend can keep an eye on you.

No question, though, that as well as being tall, this is also a broad church.

On a squally Tuesday evening, the clientele consists not just of bearded men with pints of heavy, but mothers with babies and prams, and teenagers with friends and fizzy drinks. Outside, the hail is beating a lively tattoo on the pavement and the waves are taking it out on the sea wall, but in here, it's snug and warm.

And unlike many a Scottish pub, the food is not an afterthought. Instead of the odd curly sandwich served with pickled onions, there's a big menu offering 100-plus dishes, from fish and chips (£7.29) to pasta (£4.99) to chicken tikka masala (£6.99), haggis with neeps and tatties (£5.50) and eight types of burger. Some offerings even come with a calorie count, for the waist-conscious.

And while all the usual big-name drinks brands are in stock (Foster's, Guinness etc.), there are plenty of less-mass-market Scottish ales, all prominently displayed. You can have peaty, dark Houston Warlock stout, brewed in Johnstone (4.7% ABV), or a warming winter ale called Blizzard (4.7% ABV, brewed by Sinclair, formerly Orkney and Atlas). Then there is meaty, bittersweet Jeddart Justice (4.7% ABV, Broughton of Biggar), commemorating the old, rough-and-ready Borders law that dictated that a man should be hanged first, and tried later.

Best beer of all, though, is the fragrantly powerful Mighty XP, a 6% ABV pale ale, cooked up by Old Worthy in the Isle of Skye. Plus another four or five north-of-the-border brews: a credit, this, to the West Kirk's proprietors, who aren't some small pioneering pub firm but industry giants J D Wetherspoon.

So many watering holes these days find it hard to win the hearts of local people. By contrast, with its come-unto-me prices (£7.09 for an 8oz steak plus pint), its daily promotions (Fish Friday, Chicken Wing-It Wednesday) and its message of welcome for all, the West Kirk is helping to spread the gospel of pub-going far and wide.

God bless it in its work.

Christopher Middleton, 22 February 2014

58a Sandgate, Ayr, South Ayrshire (01292 880416); www.jdwetherspoon.com/pubs/all-pubs/scotland/south-ayrshire/the-west-kirk-ayr

North-West England

The Britannia Inn
Elterwater, Cumbria

The Langdale Pikes were pretty in the sunshine, but a less ambitious walk was called for because the clouds lay low on the fells. Taking the Cumbria Way west from Skelwith Bridge, we were rewarded with a sight of Colwith Force waterfall on the River Brathay. Then, a detour of a couple of miles north to Elterwater in Langdale brought us to the Britannia Inn.

There is a maple tree on a small green in front of the whitewashed pub. A large inn sign shows a sailing ship on a choppy blue sea. On a briskly sunny day there are lots of walkers sitting outside enjoying lunch with real ales at the many chairs and tables.

Inside there is a queue to get to the small main bar with hand-pulls for several excellent beers. The delightfully named Neddy Boggle Bitter (3.6%) is smooth and pleasant. A white-painted stone road marker is depicted on the pump: apparently this scared passing horses as if there were a ghost or 'boggle' there. The Britannia Special (4.2%) is more to my taste, however, with a deep, hoppy flavour. It is brewed specially for the inn by the Coniston Brewing Company, which also has the reliable Bluebird Bitter (3.6%) on offer at the bar.

The Britannia has a back bar and dining room if you can't find space in the main bar. The food is Lake District-sourced home-made pub grub: Cumberland pâté with port sauce, Cumberland sausage on mash and onion gravy, and minted South Lakes lamb Henry. Britannia brûlée or sticky toffee pudding with hot toffee sauce might finish you off.

This was lunchtime, however, and there was more walking to do, so a selection of bread rolls with salad and a few chunky chips would have to suffice our party of intrepid (if somewhat wrinkly) hikers.

Lakeland prints and maps adorn the walls of the Britannia, which is very definitely a walker's pub. If you want to stay right in the heart of the Lake District there are nine rooms; you will be able to put your boots on in the morning and head for Grasmere or Rydal Water. Or if you are feeling energetic, Pike o' Stickle or Pavey Ark are peaks of over 2,000 feet that will reward you with magnificent views.

In Bill Birkett's excellent *Complete Lakeland Fells*, he identifies 541 separate fell tops of over 1,000 feet. I'm ticking them off and am nearly halfway there, but a good deal of the pleasure in doing so comes from visiting welcoming and homely pubs like the Britannia. Good beer, hearty food – and the company of fellow walkers with whom to discuss the merits of this ale or the pitfalls of that route up Helvellyn.

I may not manage the full set of Lake District fells – but I'm having a lot of fun trying.

Ed Jowsey, 12 September 2015

Elterwater, Ambleside, Cumbria LA22 9HP (01539 437210); thebritanniainn.com

Hole in t'Wall
Bowness-on-Windermere, Cumbria

As its name suggests, this is not an easy pub to find. Surprising really, this being the Lake District, where even the most modest attractions are signposted several times over.

To track down this 401-year-old inn, you have to turn off down a narrow little Windermere lane called Low Side, and, at the point where it meets another narrow lane called Low Fold, look sharply to the right and keep an eye out for wooden tables.

On the outer wall, there's a mural depicting Thomas Longmire, who was in charge here from 1852 to 1862, at the same time as being champion wrestler of all England ('a quiet-looking giant', observed Charles Dickens, who drank here in 1857).

Inside, the first thing that strikes you is the mass of china hanging from the ceiling; multicoloured china mugs, alongside florally-themed chamber pots. And where there aren't dangling ceramics, there are stuffed animals.

Meanwhile, down at ground level, there are fireplaces, both active with flames, and dormant and rusting, in the form of ancient stoves. Some are in the ground-floor bar, others down the little staircase in the lower Smithy Bar.

Here, a large sign bears witness to the days when this part of the pub was a forge, with the words: 'The blacksmith he did sweat in here, and slake his thirst with Hartley's beer'.

This, it turns out, is how the pub got its name. Known originally as the New Hall Inn, it became the Hole in t'Wall thanks to the gap in the brickwork that was knocked through so that the blacksmith could be served a beer while at his anvil.

These days, of course, it's not just large men with hammers who can have a pint of Hartley's. The firm's XB bitter (4.0% ABV) is a regular fixture, as are fellow ales Dizzy Blonde (a gentle 3.8%) and the slightly more urgent Unicorn (4.2%), both from Robinsons, who took over Hartley's 30 years ago.

The food is unfussy and largely un-Cumbrian (curry, cod and chips, both £9.95), with the exception of the pleasingly meaty pork pie plus Westmorland chutney (£3.95). First prize for unpretentiousness goes to the tasty, fried potato 'spirals' served in a large pile with tomato chutney (£2.95).

Despite its hideaway location, the pub gets busy in summer, as demonstrated by a rather sarcastic sheet of text left out on every table, listing all the annoying things that customers do (dither, complain, jump the queue, forget their order etc.).

It reads like one long sneer, which is a shame, since the staff are efficient and polite. Despite the notices asking you not to throw things on the fire, perhaps an exception should be made for these bits of ill-advised A4.

Christopher Middleton, 20 April 2013

Low Side, Bowness-on-Windermere, Cumbria LA23 3DH (01539 443488)

The Hest Bank Inn
Hest Bank, Lancashire

The Hest Bank Inn is the pub you would want at the end of your street. It's the sort of place where elderly locals can reel off the names of every landlord going back to their childhoods – and beyond – and who readily welcome visitors into their 'family'.

From the pub's origins in 1554, it has hosted cockfights and bare-knuckle bouts, harboured highwaymen, nourished navvies, welcomed stagecoaches and sheltered travellers. The handsome hostelry's random stonework bears traces of ancient incursions into neighbouring dwellings and stables, and it's said that the floorboards are timbers from shipwrecks.

Five separate and distinctly differing rooms mop up drinkers and diners, while the public bar is quietly laid aside for those who fancy a pint or two, a scan of the paper and another round of 'landlords' monikers'.

Hest Bank lies three miles north of Morecambe, above the eponymous bay with its fast-moving tides and treacherous quicksands, but those dangers are overcome momentarily by views of the distant Lake District to inspire the soul, and sunsets that bring an extra glow to a nightcap.

The pub garden butts up to the Lancaster Canal linking Preston with Kendal – an unusual 41-mile, lock-free coastal run where, in its commercial days, coal went one way and limestone came t'other. And there can hardly be a more relaxing pint than one supped to the tune of a narrowboat slipping in a leisurely manner past your table, followed closely by a family of ducks.

Fellow customers are a mixed bunch. Day-trippers, canalistas, cyclists, holidaymakers, recovering joggers and dog-walkers form a constant flow towards the counter and are further described by owner Robert Glenn as 'lovers, families, travellers, friends, beer drinkers and foodies'.

Robert and his wife, Susan, taught hospitality at Lancaster and Morecambe College, where they winkle out talent to develop menus that lean heavily on quality local produce. The principals in venison and beef cobbler are sourced from next-door Cumbria; the lock-keeper's platter is an assortment of the pub's own boiled ham, Morecambe-raised pork pie and Lancashire cheese; while Fleetwood platter features kiln-roasted salmon, dill herring and Morecambe Bay cockles.

Golden and fruity Thwaites Wainwright (4.1% ABV) and the lightly biting Black Sheep Best Bitter (3.8% ABV) vie for bestseller status with their well honed dependability. Red Squirrel Hopfest (3.8% ABV) offers something different and it would be wrong for our sojourn not to include Lancaster Blonde (4.1% ABV), an earthily Germanic creation advertised as 'brewed just up the road'.

On one wall of the pub, a framed photograph dated 1921 depicts the Bradford Motorcycle and Light Car Club Trial, a 100-mile round-trip that attracted 38 contestants, 'including five ladies ... who all finished the course'.

Bare-knuckle fighters wouldn't have stood a chance against Ida Pickles, Nellie Suddard and their companions.

Alastair Gilmour, 27 September 2014

2 Hest Bank Lane, Hest Bank, Lancashire LA2 6DN (01524 824339); thehestbankinn.co.uk

The Irwell Works Brewery Tap
Ramsbottom, Lancashire

Ramsbottom is a quirky place in the West Pennines, a dozen miles north of Manchester. They have a steam train, the East Lancs Railway, running through; the annual Old English Game Cock Show; a festival of chocolate and another of jigsaws; not to mention the World Black Pudding Throwing Championships, a rerun of the Wars of the Roses in which Lancashire black puddings are hurled at piles of Yorkshire ones.

The town has more than its fair share of good pubs, the Irwell Works Brewery Tap, opened in 2011, being the latest. The former Irwell Steam, Tin, Copper and Iron Works, c. 1888, has been transformed into a brewery downstairs, with a splendid pub upstairs. This latter is a one-room affair, with a hop-festooned bar and a large balcony outside for smokers, romantics and connoisseurs of urban landscapes. There's a bird's-eye view from here down on to a car park, with rolling moors in the far distance spiked with slowly churning wind turbines.

We're here for the beer and there are at least eight downstairs-brewed cask ales on offer. You can lighten the load by drinking from one-third-of-a-pint glasses, or even free pre-tasting with a smaller glass that looks like a large test tube.

A Scots gentleman next to me claimed that, where he came from, the name for this glass was a pony. This provoked one of those wonderful amiable pub arguments where no one really knows what they're talking about. 'A pony,' said someone, 'is Cockney for a fiver.' Someone else said, no, it was £500; a further opined £25 ('aka: a Napoleon. Napoleon Bony …'). The barmaid settled the discussion by saying firmly that they, the bar staff, called it a shot glass.

I took a few shots from the glasses, sniffed and sipped appreciatively, then jettisoned all organoleptic conclusions and went for the beer with the silliest name: Costa Del Salford (4.1% ABV), first brewed for a pub perched over the dubious waters of the Irwell a few miles down river, where it serves as the frontier between Salford and Manchester.

Fitzpatrick's Temperance Bar is in Rawtenstall, a few miles away: surprisingly, several of its drinks are on offer here. But the Irwell Works mixologists are bent on subtly undermining the Temperance ethos – gin with rhubarb and rosehip was one suggestion. I politely turned down the idea. Instead, I tried Iron Plate Lancashire Stout (4.4%), billed as 'a meal in itself, brewed from an old Irish recipe'. Remember that old industrial Lancashire was half Irish. It was a very fine stout.

The kitchen is a work in progress and the food is minimalist (pies, sausage rolls, crisps, nuts). The fellow next to me ordered 'a large sauvignon and a pork pie, please'.

Arthur Taylor, 26 September 2015

Irwell Street, Ramsbottom, Lancashire BL0 9YQ (01706 825019); irwellworksbrewery.co.uk

The Cemetery Hotel
Rochdale, Lancashire

L et's dispel all notions of gloom straight away. The Cemetery Hotel, although right opposite Rochdale's vast cemetery, is actually a cheerful and welcoming sort of place.

It's a home from home for Rochdale Football Club supporters on match days – one room is a shrine to the Dale, with signed shirts and historic photos of rare past triumphs on display. Away fans often turn up as well for friendly post-match analysis, banter and a few pints. A football-friendly pub may not seem the ideal place to find fine ale and civilised company, but hooligans are thin on the ground in these parts and there never seems to be any bother here.

The surroundings are hardly those of a sports bar. The impressive entrance lobby has a lovely mosaic on the floor, Art Nouveau tiles on the walls and some beautiful woodwork. That's just a foretaste.

The Cemetery, first opened in the 1860s to cater for the funeral trade, had a complete makeover in the early 1900s and it has retained most of those later glamorous features, so much so that it is listed as a precious building, not just by the Campaign for Real Ale's architectural buffs on their National Inventory of Historic Pub Interiors, but by English Heritage no less.

The cosiest room is first left. There are four elegantly numbered corners, separated by low baffle screens, each with a half circle of comfortable seats. Go for Number 2 or Number 3, because they are nearest the fire. There are notices here: 'Spouses are like fires – left untended, they will go out.' And: 'Please feel free to throw a log on the fire.'

The bar is a stand-up or perch-on-a-barstool area for serious drinking. They have six or seven cask ales which change regularly. It was good to see and taste Spotland Gold, from the Phoenix Brewery, in nearby Heywood – Spotland is Rochdale's football ground. There's another, rather more comforting notice here: 'If you think the head on your beer is too large, please tell us. We will gladly top it up.'

You wouldn't cross continents for the food, but it is perfectly fine pub grub. A huge noticeboard in the bar offers the usual suspects: pies, scampi, burgers, sausages and so on, all with copious helpings of vegetables and salad. Nothing costs more than £6.50.

A much larger room upstairs is reserved for special occasions. There's a famous medium coming up soon. The session costs £10 per person and he looks forward to 'Full audience participation in energy, glass or table movement'.

I'm not so sure about the next bit, when your man seeks to offer 'proof of loved ones on the other side'.

Well, I mean, as I said, the cemetery is just across the road.

Arthur Taylor, 5 January 2013

470 Bury Road, Rochdale, Lancashire OL11 5EU (01706 645635)

The Healey
Rochdale, Lancashire

News that a long-loved old pub has been modernised always brings out the inner curmudgeon. I loathe the damage done to pubs in recent times by 'cutting-edge' interior design consultants.

In the case of the Healey, a small end-terrace pub, the refurbishment was done recently – at vast expense – by tenants Simon and Heidi Crompton and the brewery, Robinsons of Stockport. No worries there: the Cromptons also run the Baum, Rochdale's CAMRA pub of 2013, and they clearly know their stuff. Robinsons are a long established traditional family company with some 340 pubs and a reputation for fine beers and a respect for tradition – think cask beers, shire horses and beautiful pub signs.

So, the Healey has been enlarged, buffed up and redecorated, but the old character of the place has been carefully and kindly preserved. The cottage next door is now the kitchen and the food is considerably more imaginative – in the old days it was crisps and nuts, now you can get the likes of chargrilled chicken fillets stuffed with smoked cheese and wrapped in bacon (£7.85), or roast topside of beef in a baguette with gravy, a jaw-dislocating treat at £5.15.

Best of all to my mind is the selection of three or six Lancashire cheeses (£6.95 or £11.95). There may be those of you from foreign parts who don't realise that creations such as Butler's Blacksticks Blue, Mrs Kirkham's Tasty Lancashire, Sandham's Smoked Lancashire and Inglewhite

Goats are among the finest cheeses on the planet. Here is your chance to learn.

Robinsons, with a new generation in charge, have broadened their beer portfolio. Besides the old famous favourite strong ale, Old Tom, (8.5% ABV), they now produce a spicy version, Ginger Tom, and a fruity one, Tom and Berry. And beside the original bitter, now called Unicorn, you have exotica such as Dizzy Blonde (3.8%) and Trooper (4.8%). I assumed this latter was named after one of Robinson's much-loved shire horses, but it turns out to be a creation of someone from the rock group Iron Maiden. Heavy metal beer? What will they think of next?

There are guest beers as well. Recently, they had Titanic Brewery's Last Porter Call (4.9%), a fine beer with a grim name – the pump clip maps the last place the ship sailed from. Being of a somewhat delicate disposition, I missed out on that one.

One of the good reasons for visiting the pub in the past was the splendid boules pitch at the back. Thank goodness, it's still there. No pastis and pétanque under the plane trees, granted; but French bowls and a fine draught beer under damp English greenery will do me fine.

Arthur Taylor, 14 June 2014

172 Shawclough Road, Rochdale, Lancashire OL12 6LW (01706 645453); robinsonsbrewery.com/pubs-inns-and-hotels/find-a-pub/t-z/thehealey

The Spring Inn
Rochdale, Lancashire

Several lifetimes ago, a couple of friends and I tried to get into the Spring Inn. The landlord genially suggested we should go forth and multiply – and come back when we were old enough. He was quite right: we were fifteen, and trying it on.

In those days the Spring Inn was a small, quiet country pub. A spring on the other side of the road fed a stone trough where horses used to drink before setting off with their carts up the steep hill beyond. Yes, horses and carts, the rag-and-bone man, the milkman and the occasional farmer. It was a long time ago.

Today, the pub is updated, expanded and modernised, and ticks a lot of boxes. You can drink at the bar, where there are hooks to hang your coat – I like that. There is an alcove, dressed up as a boardroom, with old cheques, invoices and letters on the wall, a vast restaurant in a conservatory at the back and acres of garden.

Best of all, there is the most palatial taproom I've ever seen, with a smart pool table and a splendid darts arena.

If you look carefully here, you can see an old photograph of the pub as it was when I was so cruelly turned away.

The Middleton brewers J.W. Lees own the place, so their beers predominate. The vin de pays of the stable is Lees Bitter, 4% ABV, which has been made to the same recipe, with Goldings hops, since 1828, when the brewery was founded. These days, with the sixth generation of assorted Lees in charge, there are more beers from which to choose. I'm fond of MPA (Manchester Pale Ale), 3.7%, which is made with Liberty and Mount Hood hops and, therefore, has that biscuity taste.

The invention of MPA a couple of years ago is a bold attempt to stake claim to the cultural identity of Manchester, now that the city's iconic beer, Boddingtons bitter, is a pale, insipid shadow of its former self. 'Boddies' used to be so ferociously hopped that it became a near-death experience for anyone trying it for the first time. MPA is the right colour, but not so fierce on the tonsils.

This was a typical English summer's day, with black low cloud, endless rain and November temperatures. You need comfort food and there is plenty of it. I go for pork and smoked bacon sausages and mash, with fresh garden peas, at £8. It arrives on a dazzling white plate the size of a washing-up bowl and is beautifully set out, like a Rembrandt still life. Best of all, there is a jug of flavoursome onion gravy, which turns out to be as good as, if not better than, mine.

Arthur Taylor, 15 August 2015

83 Broad Lane, Rochdale, Lancashire OL16 4PR (01706 633529); springinn.co.uk

The Red Lion
Littleborough, Lancashire

The Red Lion presents a solid, four-square, mid-19th-century stone façade with a fetching fringe of ivy. It stands close to Littleborough railway station, at the beginning of the long road to Blackstone Edge and the Lancashire/Yorkshire border.

In bold gold letters on the wall, it is announced that Wilsons Beers are sold. There's a fine swinging sign, an angular heraldic lion in faded red, with Wilsons written on it. Just as you go in, you glimpse a ceramic plaque which announces proudly 'Wilsons Ales, brewed since 1834'. A bit odd that. Wilsons (Newton Heath), Manchester Brewery vanished decades ago.

More oddity. A spiky handwritten note on a ragged piece of paper by the door says: 'Dogs on a lead welcome'. Next to it, another message reads: 'Sorry. No children'. Just inside you note: 'We serve drinks, not drunks'.

You're spoilt for choice as you stride the main corridor towards the bar.

To the right, there's a small parlour which reminds me of my granny's immaculate front parlour, around about 1960. To the left is a much larger room with comfortable seating. Beyond the bar, you'll spot a fine games room with immaculate pool table and a cabinet full of trophies and a large-screen television. To the left, there's a smaller, simpler room, for darts.

This is a pub, then, which caters effortlessly for a wide range of customers, as many pubs used to do. The youngsters head for the games rooms, the oldsters for the parlour, a mixed crowd goes to the concert room. The dogs tend to rest under chairs. The music played quietly in the background presents a challenge best tackled by those of a certain age – how many hits from the Fifties and Sixties can you recognise?

There are three regular beers: Timothy Taylor's Landlord, Lees Bitter and Red Lion Bitter. The latter turns out to be a house beer created by the Phoenix Brewery, Heywood. The beer costs £1.60 a pint. You can have a pint of mixed, Red Lion Bitter plus Black Bee, a honey porter made by the same brewery, for the same price. There are three guest beers, the most expensive of which costs £2.50.

Almost every pub you enter these days smells of cooking. Not this one. The only nourishment available comprises traditional thirst-inducing pub snacks – crisps, salted peanuts, pork scratchings, cheesy biscuits.

It should also be noted – as a disadvantage or not, according to taste – that the place has been described as a 'dead zone' for mobile phones.

The Red Lion is a wonderful all-our-yesterdays pub. Actually, it goes back to the 17th century, according to records kept in a cardboard box by the long-time landlord here. More research needed, I feel. I'll have another pint of mixed, please.

Arthur Taylor, 3 August 2013

6 Halifax Road, Littleborough, Lancashire OL15 0HB (01706 378195)

The Swan
Dobcross, Greater Manchester

Question: the swinging sign outside definitely announces The Swan, but there's a window etched with the name Kings Arms and locals refer to the place as the 'Top House'. What's going on? Answer: it is the Swan, it was the Kings Arms and it is almost at the top of an ankle-cracking steep road up to Dobcross village. The 'Bottom House', aka The Woolpack, at the foot of the hill, is, alas, no more: axed a year or so ago.

The Swan, rescued from near closure by locals Michael Powis and Tim Newbold about a year before that, is very much alive and well. They've opened up and spruced up the place and laid out the welcome mat for Dobcrossers and foreigners alike.

It's the current Marston's Pub of the Year, no mean achievement since the company runs more than 2,000 places of one sort and another. The conglomerate has taken over many breweries, so their portfolio is a brewers' Valhalla – a roll-call of beer heroes ancient and modern, including Banks's of the West Midlands, Jennings of Cumbria, Brakspears and Wychwood of Oxfordshire and Ringwood of Hampshire.

There are usually five cask beers on offer here. I spotted Marston's Pedigree (4.5% ABV), an old favourite of mine from years back. Beer writers wax eloquently about its properties – biscuits, nuts, apple and grapefruit, not to mention a hint of the infamous 'Burton Snatch', a whiff of sulphurous burnt matches. Not sure about some of this cornucopia, but it is a fine beer.

The walls of the three rooms are full of pictorial reminders of local legends – the Whit Friday Quickstep Competition, a historic brass band festival in springtime; the Longwood Thump, a rushcart and morris dancers' cavalcade in summer, and Yanks Weekend, an annual celebration of the Second World War film *Yanks*, which was shot in and around the village in 1978 (there was some consternation when a couple of extreme heritage enthusiasts turned out in full SS uniform).

The function room upstairs plays host to an astonishing array of frolics and fun and serious stuff. They include a folk club, jazz concerts, theatrical performances, comedy, poetry, small-scale opera and much more besides. The noticeboard by the front door is always a delight. I liked the sound of the 'Saddleworth Tour de Tweed, a Vintage Bicycle Ride for Ladies and Gentlemen'. On closer inspection, it looked very much like a leisurely pub crawl on two wheels.

Arthur Taylor, 12 April 2014

1 The Square, Dobcross, Saddleworth, Greater Manchester OL3 5AA (01457 873451); theswandobcross.com

The Britons Protection
Manchester

Here are women in shawls, toffs in toppers, weeping children in rags. That's Manchester for you. Or at least that was Manchester in 1819, when the authorities reacted to a mass demand for universal suffrage by unleashing the cavalry to kill fifteen protesters and injure between 400 and 700. Four murals in a tiled passageway at the Britons Protection offer a graphic depiction of what became known as the Peterloo Massacre.

Some terrified demonstrators sought sanctuary in this pub, which had then been up and running for thirteen years. Hence the odd name. Rather than pondering whether there should be an apostrophe in 'Britons', and whether it should go before or after the S, perhaps we should call in for a pint and a pie while reflecting on the sacrifices made to give us a vote that some nowadays tell us is a waste of time.

The pies are imported from a butcher in nearby Wythenshawe and if my steak and kidney is anything to go by, they're much improved by a jug of rich gravy made upstairs. The rest of the menu of standard pub tucker is available from noon–2pm and has long gone by the time concerts have finished at the Bridgewater Hall across the road.

Members of the Hallé Orchestra are frequent visitors. It would seem that performing Berlioz or Beethoven can work up the sort of thirst that once raged among workers in long-defunct cotton mills.

'We have fifteen pints of Jennings lined up for the

musicians at the end of each concert,' says manager Allan Hudd. That's Jennings Cumberland Ale (4% ABV), brewed at Cockermouth, 129 miles away. Distance from brewery is listed here as well as strength of beer.

Among the regulars are Robinson's Unicorn from Stockport (4.3% and 6.9 miles) and Outstanding Blond, a pale yet hefty 4.5% from Bury (9.8 miles) with citrusy undertones and a satisfyingly bitter finish.

All the beers are in peak condition, but whisky is the *specialité de la maison*. Over 300 are available, and Alan, a former cocktail barman whose Manhattans would pass muster with Don Draper, has become an enthusiast. For my untutored palate he recommends Dalwhinnie 15, a smoky single malt, and the more complex Johnnie Walker Green Label, another fifteen-year-old that's better undiluted.

Having seen off the chasers, I'm feeling even more warmly disposed towards this bar with its gold-embossed ceiling and its bust of David seeming to peer around the Irish whiskeys and gaze longingly at the pickled eggs.

As for that tiled passageway, it leads to a suntrap beer garden. In Manchester! On the way it passes two carpeted and curtained snugs, offering Britons who require it some privacy – with, one hopes, no need of protection.

Chris Arnot, 19 April 2014

50 Great Bridgewater Street, Manchester M1 5LE (0161 236 5895)

The New Oxford
Salford, Manchester

A long time ago, towards the end of the last century, I and a group of like-minded friends used to sneak off from the Granada TV studios for an extended lunch hour down the pub. We went gaming and gambling, which wasn't as dissipated as it might sound – we played pub games and whoever lost paid for the next round.

Different pubs hosted different games. One had a fine table football set-up, another, a couple of battered classic American pinball machines, a third a palatial dartboard. Then there was the Oxford, a small two-roomed house down in Salford, which had a brand new pool table, something of a novelty in those days.

The place didn't have much else to offer. It was shabby and dusty and sold indifferent beer. On one occasion, I was put off a masterful final shot on the black by a mischief of mice that scuttled across my feet.

Spool forward a lifetime and the Oxford has become the New Oxford, now billed as a 'Continental Real Ale Bar'. The contrast is extraordinary. Outside every windowsill is decked with flowers; inside, the place is spick and span, with everything polished within an inch of life.

It sells a huge range of British cask beers, a dozen when we were there. I counted four draught ciders. There's a chalk board occupying almost the whole of one wall, listing Belgian beers available in bottle and on draught.

The Belgian influence is very strong – there are Belgian beer mats, Belgian beer advertisements, a leaflet advertising the virtues of a Bruges estaminet and even a life-size (but not leaking) Manneken Pis statue, as seen, photographed and endlessly giggled over in Brussels.

The New Oxford collects and displays scores of awards, including a gem, a Pub Award from the All-Party Parliamentary Beer Group, signed by Hazel Blears, who is a born and bred Salfordian and local MP. Proof at last that these people do something useful with their time at Westminster.

So, we had a pint of Riverhead Leggers' Light (3.6%) and another of Lancaster Lemon Grass (4%), both fine beers. We had egg and chips (£4.50) – everything comes with chips, so not everything has changed.

The weather was good, so we went and sat outside underneath the flower baskets with another pint. There was an old chap there, with a wrinkled face and an earring, rolling his own cigarette with shaky hands. I was beginning to worry – was this really the place I remembered? He pointed above his head to the ancient faded pub sign – and there it was, the original sign, never removed: 'The Oxford', creaking in the wind, a bit like me.

Arthur Taylor, 18 April 2015

11 Bexley Square, Salford, Manchester M3 6DB (0161 832 7082); thenewoxford.com

The Old Boat House
Astley, Greater Manchester

The next best thing to messing about in boats is watching other people messing about in boats, with a consolatory pint in your hand. You can do this at The Old Boat House, which has been here by the Bridgewater Canal since the late 18th century. The pub was first known as the Hope and Anchor, then became the Boat House and then, feeling its age in the Sixties, was renamed The Old Boat House.

It was originally a boatmen's pub and there was extensive stabling for the horses that hauled the boats. When Astley Green Colliery, a few hundred yards away, was grafting at full stretch from 1912 to 1970, the boats, by now motorised, were delivering coal to waterside power stations. Now the visitors mooring up at the pub are civilians, with pleasure boats of all shapes and sizes.

The pub is much enlarged from the old days. There is a fine public bar on one side, and a clutter of small rooms has been opened up into one large space on the other. At the end of this part is a bit that feels boatish – it has a planked floor, wooden ceiling and walls, and a nice mix of furniture. An old josser outside told me that this was the original pub. Incidentally, if you are interested in the history of a pub, I've found it useful to go outside to the smoking area. The old regulars can't kick the habit and so are available for interview when they pop out for a drag.

The food here is excellent. Try this for size: the mixed grill, which will set you back £11.75, includes steak, gammon, Cumberland sausage, lamb cutlet, fried egg, black pudding, mushrooms, tomatoes and onion rings. I usually go for one of their curries, which come with pilau rice and proper oily, hot, burn-your-fingers poppadoms. The small portions, at £5.75, are large enough for me.

On the beer front, there is Ruddles County from the Greene King stable and Timothy Taylor's Landlord from Keighley. They're decent beers, of course, especially the Landlord, but I tend to look out for the guests. With 1,200 breweries in the country these days, there are plenty to try out. I struck lucky the other week with Red Dawn 3.7%, a dark mild, brewed by the Red Squirrel brewery from far-off Hertfordshire.

I spent the early years of my drinking apprenticeship drinking mild in the taproom for economy's sake, so this was a Proustian moment. This one is lush, malty, bit of biscuit, bit of nut and just delicious.

It pains me to say this, but nostalgia is a thing of the past, and I think Squirrel Dawn is better than the milds of my old days.

Arthur Taylor, 11 October 2014

Higher Green Lane, Astley, Tyldesley, Greater Manchester M29 7JB (01942 883300); oldboathouseastley.co.uk

The Swan with Two Nicks
Little Bollington, Cheshire

Park Lane – the Cheshire version – is a narrow, winding, hedged-in rural road which eventually delivers you to the Swan with Two Nicks. A few yards further on, the road comes to an abrupt halt – there's a narrow pedestrian footbridge over the cascading River Bollin and then, on the far side, a private car park.

If you use satnav and the postcode to find the pub, this is where you end up, on the wrong side of the river without a paddle, as it were. I do enjoy it when the new technology stuffs things up.

Back in 1745, the pub was known as Bollington Tenement No 17, 'a dwelling known as the Swan Alehouse', part of the estate of Dunham Massey Hall, property of the earls of Stanford and Warrington. Nowadays, improvements all around, the estate belongs to the National Trust and the pub is splendidly independent.

I like to think that my favourite spot, the small simple flag-floored room, just a step down from the bar, is the original alehouse, although it is now a small part of a very much larger and grander place, including a restaurant the size of an airship hangar.

There are at least seven cask ales on offer, including a house beer from the Coach House Brewery, Warrington called – would you believe – The Swan with Two Nicks, as well as several choices from the Dunham Massey brewery.

To help make up your mind, take what they call a bar flight (a wooden tray bearing three third-of-a-pint glasses each filled with a different brew, £3.80).

Food is the big number here. It ranges from a simple sandwich to the dizzy heights of pan-seared pigeon breast with bacon and wholegrain mustard mash, and a cranberry and red wine jus (£11.95).

I chose the Cromer dressed crab, with a salad and warm baguette (£13.95). Extravagant, I know, for pub grub, but if there's dressed crab on offer, I can't resist. (When the creature is *au naturel* and you need a bank of surgical instruments to crack open all the bits, and a bib to stop dribbling it down your front, I'm more reticent.)

The pub is doggy friendly, up to a point. 'Why not treat your furry friend with dog biscuits and water from the bar?' says one notice. However, 'Please do not have dogs on the furniture, unless on a dog blanket,' says another.

There are always lots of children here too, although I didn't see any notices suggesting how they should behave.

I had heard that this was a mobile-free zone. Good news. The barmaid said no, reception was possible, but 'very patchy'. Ah well: can't win them all.

Arthur Taylor, 6 September 2014

Park Lane, Little Bollington, Altrincham, Cheshire WA14 4TJ (0161 928 2914); swanwithtwonicks.co.uk

The Fiddle I'th Bag Inn
Burtonwood, Cheshire

It's always cheering to find English eccentricity alive and well. Step through the door of the Fiddle I'th Bag Inn and I defy you not to get an attack of the giggles.

You pass, for example, two thigh-high Belisha beacons and espy a statue of Rupert the Bear, a Hollywood model in a black swimsuit, a pile of life-jackets, a stuffed chimpanzee on a settee and much more besides.

The place is crammed from floor to ceiling with what might be described as antiques, memorabilia, bygones or junk, according to taste. There are coats and jackets, hats, helmets, stuffed fish, fishing rods, old cameras, Victorian samplers, film posters, ancient books, magazines – the list is endless.

It's tricky to see what beers are available because the peninsula bar is covered in piles of old tobacco tins and Dinky toys, and there is a miner's lamp and a Bill and Ben Flowerpot Man puppet dangling at eye level.

But make no mistake, this is a proper pub. There are three local cask beers on offer. They're popular, and they change frequently, so the landlady always offers three tiny glasses full of the day's offerings, to taste and select. Frodsham Gold (4.1%) was our favourite and Ringway Session (3.8%) from Stockport was a close second, so we tried both, in pint form.

There is a large, no-nonsense menu. We had the homemade steak and onion pie, with baked potatoes, peas and salad (£6.25).

I'm something of a connoisseur of steak and ale pie –

and this was wonderful. The ale was Theakston, apparently, but the landlady said she used different ales, according to availability. The pies and puddings menu would provide choice enough for most, but you could aim high and have a T-bone steak for £12.25.

Burtonwood was an American air force and army base from 1942–94, so there are tales to be told and, naturally, there is a wartime flavour to some of the décor. The background music was definitely Forties vintage – a bit before my time, but I did recognise Tommy Dorsey's trombone, Glenn Miller schmaltz, George Formby's ukulele and the Gracie Fields classic 'The Thing-Ummy-Bob' (that's going to win the war).

If you don't know what I'm talking about, improve your education and catch this latter on YouTube – it's simply brilliant.

The rather fine pub sign depicts a polished violin being slipped inside a blue velvet bag. Nothing could be further from the truth. The fiddle and the bag was a primitive agricultural instrument, worked by a rod, for sowing seed. Lo and behold, they have one of those, too, hanging directly above the bar.

Arthur Taylor, 23 May 2015

Alder Lane, Burtonwood, Warrington, Cheshire WA5 4BJ (01925 225442)

Gallagher's Pub & Barbers
Birkenhead

A man goes to the bar and a man goes to the barber's. At Gallagher's you can do both. Pub and barber's shop share the same late-Georgian building near the waterfront in Birkenhead.

No sooner have I savoured a very acceptable swig of Trapper's Hat (3.8% ABV), brewed at Brimstage in the Wirral, than I'm called through for my appointment with a cut-throat razor. The man wielding it, landlord-cum-barber Franky Gallagher, is drinking nothing stronger than coffee. 'That's why my hand's shaking,' he beams.

Oh, that Scouse sense of humour. Perhaps it also accounts for the Sweeney Todd accessory I see as a hot towel engulfs my face – an empty cabinet for keeping pies hot.

'We fill it on Saturday lunchtimes,' says Franky after removing the hot towel and setting to with the badger brush. Gallagher's has become a pre-match beacon for discerning football supporters from far and wide. 'The Coventry City fans were great when they came to play Tranmere,' Franky goes on, dexterously manoeuvring that fearsome blade under my nose. 'They ate all the pies in fifteen minutes and seemed to love the place.'

Who can blame them? Franky and his wife, Sue, barbers both, took over a derelict pub called the Dispensary a few years ago and transformed it into something special. The drinking area is predominantly dark wood relieved by a vaulted ceiling of decorative glass over the bar itself. Walls are covered with pictures of ocean-going liners on the Mersey, submarines made at nearby Cammell Laird and memorabilia from Franky's days as an Irish Guardsman.

A piano regularly bursts into life under the skilled fingers of Peter the Pianist: Rachmaninov one minute, 'Roll out the Barrel' the next. And there are bi-monthly poetry nights featuring the Roger McGoughs and Adrian Henris *de nos jours* in the cocktail bar upstairs.

As for the beer, you can see why this was CAMRA's Merseyside Pub of the year in 2011 and 2012. The moisturiser soothing my newly-smoothed chops does not impair my reacquaintance with the fruity yet bitter-edged Trapper's Hat, nor the slightly weaker yet just as full-flavoured Windermere Pale (3.5% ABV) from the Hawkshead Brewery in Cumbria. From across the Pennines comes Ossett's pale yet heavily-hopped White Rat (4.0% ABV); from across the river, Liverpool Organic Brewery's Honey Blond, 4.5% ABV and not as cloying as it sounds.

A young man has just slipped into the barber's carrying a pint and asking for a Brad Pitt. More popular than a David Beckham, I'm told, perhaps because Beckham changes the length and lay of his locks more often than some men change their razor blades. But a good pint will never go out of fashion at Gallagher's.

Chris Arnot, 22 March 2014

20 Chester Street, Birkenhead CH41 5DQ (0151 649 9095); gallagherspubwirral.com

The Yew Tree
Bunbury, Cheshire

The Yew Tree, originally called the Crewe Arms, is a Victorian fantasia on the theme of a black-and-white half-timbered medieval house – but there's a twist. At the front, high up, where only a sharp-eyed architectural connoisseur would spot them, are four odd designs, each made up of the punts, or bases, of seven champagne bottles. According to an expert, this is a typical piece of whimsy from the Earl of Crewe's buildings. Did he drink the bubbly himself and kindly donate the 28 empties, I wonder?

As the Crewe Arms, the place fell on hard times and almost closed for good. It was rescued by Jon and Lindsay Cox, who reopened the pub as the Yew Tree in the summer of 2010, after an extensive refurbishment. Today, the pub merits extravagant praise in all the guide books you care to name, for good food, good beer and good vibes. How did they do it?

'First, make it a pleasant place to come to,' says Jon. That meant opening up four rather dark rooms and freshening up the décor. 'Next, engage with the whole community' – Jon wants local tractor drivers and cowmen to feel just as much at home here as the *Hollyoaks* set.

The policy is clearly working. There were examples of both at the bar when we called. One group around a table shared a handsome-looking bottle of red wine. A chap in a battered cloth cap at the bar nursed a pint, while his dog had its own bowl at his feet.

Good beer is vital, in fact, in spite of the fine reputation for dining here, 50% of trade is 'wet' – folk come here for the beer. Stonehouse Station Bitter, from Oswestry (3.9% ABV) is the house beer and very pleasant it is too. There are up to seven guest beers, constantly changing, and Jon is keen on seasonal beers. They also serve BrewDog craft beers including the devilish Tokyo Imperial Stout – fruity, complex and fully 18.2% ABV; on the lighter side, in hue at least, there's always Vedett Extra Blond (5.2% ABV), a clean, malty pilsner-style beer from Belgium, and Erdinger Weissbier, one of the tastiest German wheat beers (5.3% ABV) on draught.

The food is seasonal, too. We were there in the winter and game was on the menu. 'Are Yew Game?' questioned the chalkboard, archly. I had the game pie (£11.50) which had partridge, pheasant and mallard in it, together with peas and chips fried in beef fat – the only way to go if you are a chip. My wife took the game terrine (£7) which was wrapped in smoked bacon and came with a bloomer and home-made chutney.

It was Jon who told me the secret of the wine-bottle décor. He has a taste for whimsy as well. In one room there's the head and shoulders of a stuffed fox – in the room next door, you can see its hindquarters and brush.

Arthur Taylor, 4 January 2014

Long Lane, Spurstow, Bunbury, Cheshire CW6 9RD (01829 260274); theyewtreebunbury.com

West Midlands

The Devonshire Arms
Burton upon Trent

'**Y**ou'd make a rubbish arsonist,' the woman perched on a stool at the counter says with a laugh as the barmaid attempts to get the coal fire to light. Moments later, it finally catches and the barmaid utters a small cry of triumph – but there's more work to be done: 'It's the bigger one in the back room I've got to worry about now,' she says.

Having a proper fire is part of the great British pub tradition and the one in the front bar of the Devonshire is a classic example: metal grate, coals glowing and the whole room warming up. The effect is homely and comforting, adding to the welcoming ambience of the room, with old photos on the wall, embossed mirrors and a solid wooden bar counter.

The Devonshire is a traditional pub in the best possible way, and barmaids and barmen have been lighting fires in its brace of rooms since the middle of the 19th century. This is a pub that has weathered the many changes the former capital of brewing has gone through. Now, it has settled into its cosy role as a popular neighbourhood local, not far from the station, and I am equally settled in my seat with a glass of beer in front of me.

John Barleycorn rules here and at the bar there are five cask beers, all made by the pub's owner, Burton Bridge Brewery, a brisk ten-minute walk away close to the Trent. On offer are Damson Porter, a fruity dark beer with a cappuccino-coloured head of foam; the gleaming golden ale Stairway to Heaven; and the classic XL Bitter. I ask for a pint of Festival Ale, which at 5.5% is a potent potation but irresistible in its charm. It's dark gold in colour and bittersweet on the palate, finishing with the kind of intense dry finish that sets you up for a further swig.

Another tradition roundly kept in the Devonshire is the food. No pan-fried this and that here, but locally made pork pies, sturdy and robust, with three different pork-centric combinations: pork and black pudding, pork and Stilton, and pork and chorizo. I opt for the third and am hooked from the first bite. The pastry is crumbly and soft, while the meat is juicy and smoky – Spain meets Staffordshire and all get on famously.

Meanwhile, the woman at the bar, who has only just moved to Burton, continues her chat with the barmaid. 'This is my type of pub and I felt welcome here as soon as I came in,' she says. I can echo that sentiment.

At the Devonshire, you are brought face to face with the great attraction of the British pub: it provides a home from home, with warmth, comfort, life and, of course, good beer. Talking of which, my glass is empty and there's time for another.

Adrian Tierney-Jones, 7 March 2015

86 Station Street, Burton upon Trent DE14 1BT (01283 562392); thedevonshire.co.uk

Hail to the Ale
Wolverhampton

The taxi driver is still sceptical as we pass through one of Wolverhampton's more salubrious suburbs. 'I ain't never seen a pub in Pendeford Avenue,' he maintains.

'Well, you have now,' I respond, pointing to what admittedly looks more like a corner shop. Which is exactly what it was until a few years ago – a furniture shop, and before that a post office. Hail to the Ale is one of a new breed of micropubs offering restricted fare during restricted hours in a restricted space. No hot food, lager, Guinness, spirits, cocktails or alcopops. And nothing at all from 5pm sharp on a Sunday until the same time on Thursday when it reopens for five hours.

I arrive just before 5.30pm on a Friday. Already the room is humming with unimpeded conversation. Did I mention that there's no music? No television or gaming machines, either.

Suits me, to be honest, although it might not suit my wife – she's a wine drinker, and that constituency is not well served. Still, she's not here and I am, relishing the thought that these small-scale ale and cider houses can only enhance our stricken high streets at a time when nearly 30 pubs a week are apparently closing down.

Once across the threshold, there's no doubting that this is a pub – bare boards, dangling tankards, barrels doubling as tables, and walls bedecked by beer mats advertising the diverse range of seasonal beers produced by Morton microbrewery.

Gary Morton brews on an industrial estate three miles away. 'He started in our garage, three miles the other way,' says his wife, Angela, 'and before I knew it, he'd taken over the airing cupboard as well.'

She's pulling me a pint of Scrummage, a well-balanced amber ale weighing in at 4.7% ABV, a suitably hefty elbow-bender for the Rugby World Cup. Belgian malt and New Zealand hops, if you please. There are guest beers from small local breweries and a draught cider.

Prices are reasonable – not much more than £2.80 a pint. Don't be taken in, however, by the sign offering 'chicken in the basket' for £1.20. This being the Black Country, they have their own version of that one-time pub 'classic' – a packet of crushed crisps with a pickled egg stuffed inside.

Apart from crisps and pickles, there are pork pies and pork scratchings. 'He loves the scratchings,' says a genial gent at the bar as his dog sets about his second bag. 'I think they've got rocket fuel in them. He can't half run.'

My 'locally sourced' pork pie is heavy on the meat, light on the jelly and short in the pastry – a tasty counterweight to the Scrummage. I've squeezed on to the only available seat, a handsomely carved wooden settle, opposite a recently retired prep-school head teacher and his wife. 'I'm trying a half of bitter for the first time,' she says. Her preferred tipple, it transpires, is the occasional glass of champagne: not an option here.

Chris Arnot, 10 October 2015

2 Pendeford Avenue, Claregate, Tettenhall, Wolverhampton WV6 9EF (07846 562910); hailtothealemicropub.co.uk; open Thu/Fri 5–10pm, Sat noon–10pm, Sun noon–5pm

The Great Western
Wolverhampton

Like the Rovers Return, the Great Western stands on a cobbled street close to a railway arch. The accents inside owe more to the West Midlands than the western side of the Pennines, however. And during my visit at least, the clientele veered more towards Ken Barlow than Kevin Webster.

One customer was bent over the *Telegraph* cryptic crossword in the tiled front bar, while a couple at the next table were discussing Renaissance art over bowls of pumpkin soup.

Abandon your Black Country stereotypes, all ye who enter here. Then call for a pint of Holden's Black Country Bitter or, if you're lucky, Batham's from nearby Brierley Hill. Alas, the Batham's was 'still settling' when I called in. 'We're allowed four barrels a week and once it's gone, it's gone,' says manager Kate Williamson.

Gone but not forgotten, if my experience of that deceptively pale yet powerfully hopped nectar is anything to go by. Still, the Holden's range, including a chocolatey mild and the citrusy Golden Glow, offers a more than dependable alternative.

As for food, I have an equally dependable motto: when in Rome, eat pasta; when in Wolverhampton, eat pork. Sound judgement in this case. Chunks of hot and succulent meat oozed their juices into a necessarily substantial soft, white bap.

Other local delicacies on a very reasonably-priced lunch-time menu include faggots and peas as well as bacon with 'grey' peas, the grey ones being very much an acquired taste.

The pub is sited in the lee of Wolverhampton station, and more than justifies missing a train or three. For railway 'enthusiasts' it must be a place of pilgrimage. Photographs abound of steam trains chugging in and out on the long-deceased Great Western low-level line, and there's a 1922 map of GWR freight routes above an iron fireplace of similar vintage, almost certainly cast in a local foundry.

A dartboard elbows its way between more 'steamy' photographs (don't get excited) in a snug with another open fire. Access is just off a long, narrow room with polished floorboards and an even narrower passageway dominated by a huge advertisement for Palethorpe's Sausages.

It comes as a surprise to find a conservatory at the far end – haunt of the local business community judging by the collar-and-tie count. There's a piano that comes to life on party nights, I'm told, and a wall dedicated to Wolverhampton Wanderers. A framed front page celebrates the last time they lifted the FA Cup. It's dated 7 May 1960.

The glass roof reveals a landscape dominated by overhead power lines – a depressing reminder that it's time to bid farewell to the Great Western and reconnect with Virgin Trains.

Chris Arnot, 9 November 2013

Sun Street, Wolverhampton WV10 0DG (01902 351090)

The Shakespeare
Birmingham

There are two Shakespeares in the middle of Birmingham. One is just around the corner from the bewildering warren that is New Street station. The other, described here, involves a trek across town to the point where the city centre bleeds away into the Jewellery Quarter.

Goldsmiths and silversmiths slaked well-earned thirsts in this Victorian gem for a century or so. They were joined eventually by labourers building four-lane highways, such as the one beyond the front window.

Today the Shakespeare is more upmarket, a welcome haven from the traffic. Lunchtime sunshine is spilling through that window and gleaming on a dazzling brass table near the door. The wooden floor is equally well polished, and the handsome bar-back is stocked with a wide range of wines and whiskies.

Here are all the hallmarks of a Nicholson's pub, although Nicholson's is now part of Mitchells & Butlers, which has its HQ just beyond what must surely be the most pleasantly unexpected pub garden in central Birmingham – an oasis within a haven. M&B was once a brewery whose products dominated this city.

Mercifully, the Shakespeare offers a choice of much finer draught beers than their once-ubiquitous Brew XI, all dispensed from handsome wood-and-brass handpumps and all in tip-top condition. Among them is Ubu, at 4.5% the strongest of three lip-smacking ales from the Purity Brewery in rural Warwickshire. Then there's a well-balanced 4% pale ale, brewed for Nicholson's by St Austell. The other regular is Doom Bar, needless to say, and there are three guests, including an American IPA and, believe it or not, a 'chilli and chocolate' stout.

'It's bostin',' says a corpulent Black Countryman at the bar. Pretty good, in other words. I'm prepared to take his word for it until persuaded to try a small sample by one of the bar staff. Mmmm: much better than I expected.

And the 'ocean pie' (£10.50), selected from an extensive menu, is every bit as good as I expected. Chunks of salmon, smoked haddock and king prawns swim in a creamy cheese-and-leek sauce beneath the choppy surface of lightly browned mashed potato.

At this point, a party of fifteen pensioners files in and heads for the snug-like back bar, with its studded leather seats and splendid marble fireplace. They've been on a tour of the nearby Coffin Works and its museum. And, no, they haven't been putting down deposits. The former factory once made the handles for Churchill's coffin. As for the pensioners, they're members of the University of the Third Age, their thirst for knowledge unquenched by time.

My own thirst – for ale – well quenched, it's time to head back to the station. It was worth the walk.

Chris Arnot, 4 April 2015

Summer Row, Birmingham B3 1JJ (0121 236 8702); nicholsonspubs.co.uk/restaurants/eastandwestmidlands/theshakespeareinnsummerrowbirmingham

The Wellington
Birmingham

'This place is hallowed ground,' says a cheery chap, one of a sociable quartet of drinkers sitting around the table in a corner of the Wellington's long lounge bar. He takes a deep draught from his glass of Oakham Ales' boldly hopped golden ale Citra (think mangoes and grapefruit with bracing biscuity notes) and continues with his eulogy. 'We travel here from Sutton Coldfield at least once a week. This is a true pub.' His companions utter their approval with lifted glasses.

The English public house at its best is about conviviality in the company of similarly inclined folk along with a few ales, and the Wellington is an outstanding example of this rich mixture. On the weekday evening I visit, it is lively and buoyant, bustling with young and old, men and women.

This is a pub that engages the senses: flashes of gold, bronze and copper dart about the chunky wooden bar as glasses of ale are dispensed and the hum of conversation rustles around the bar. After-work stories are exchanged and the merits of the nearby Christmas market discussed ('unimpressed' is one of the less bruising comments uttered). There's even a game of darts going on in another part of the bar.

The Wellington stands on a corner in the Bennetts Hill area of the city centre, a solid-looking 19th-century town house. Once through the door you step into a bar whose walls are covered with flock wallpaper while the carpet is a swirl of caramel browns. The design is reminiscent of a provincial hotel lounge, but there's an honesty about this interior that makes a refreshing change from the so-hip-that-it's-not-hip minimalism of a self-styled 'Bar + Kitchen'.

One glance at the bar, where sixteen handpumps are lined up like ships of the line, provides an instant answer to anyone curious as to the pub's appeal. Cask is king here with the selection listed on a screen hanging next to the bar. As soon as one cask finishes and another replaces it, the screen's information changes – it's a bit like being at New Street station. There's no food (unless you count pork scratchings), though customers are encouraged to bring in their own and the pub provides plates and cutlery.

And the beers? The aforementioned Citra is one favourite, but there are also selections from Black Country Brewery (who own the pub), Wye Valley, Ossett and my particular tipple, Wreckage from Titanic Brewery. This is a big hitter of a winter ale, brimming with fruit (think currants, raisins, oranges) and a hint of Christmas spice. It's rich and elegant on the palate and its dry finish encourages me to take another sip. However, there's just one thing, at 7.2% this is an aptly named beer to be treated with respect. After all I am on hallowed ground.

Adrian Tierney-Jones, 6 December 2014

37 Bennetts Hill, Birmingham B2 5SN (0121 200 3115); thewellingtonrealale.co.uk

The Prince of Wales
Moseley, Birmingham

Keith Marsden, British Institute of Innkeepers Licensee of the Year, is sporting a natty straw hat and a colourful short-sleeved shirt. He looks like a man dressed for the beach rather than a pub garden in Birmingham. He also looks like someone who should have a cigar clamped in his chops.

'Funny you should mention that,' he says and leads the way to the Cigar Bar, one of several huts hereabouts. It's Thursday evening and the Prince of Wales' resident Ukulele Club is warming up for its rehearsal night in a neighbouring hut.

Members sometimes serenade the sizeable crowd gathered under a vast canopy. 'In winter we have a huge log-burner called Bruno out here,' says Keith, who used to be in brand marketing for Coca-Cola.

The brand of cigar that he's holding up reverentially, as though it recently rolled off a virgin's thigh, is a Cohiba. 'That would set you back around 50 quid,' he confides. Lesser brands start at around a tenner. Aficionados can relax on comfortable settees and gaze through the haze while also enjoying a pint. 'Or a brandy?' 'Rum's better with cigars,' Keith assures me.

Funny he should mention that. Another hut offers rum-based cocktails. There's also a well-stocked wine hut.

You can tell we're in 'Moseley village', as the residents call this, the Islington of Brum. The only food you can get at the pub, mind you, is from another hut dealing mainly in burgers and hot dogs – and that's just from Thursdays to Sundays.

'There are plenty of restaurants round here,' Keith shrugs. 'This is essentially a boozer.'

Funny he should mention that. Since heading along a tiled passageway to the garden, I'd almost forgotten that there's a pub back there. Not just any old pub either. The Prince has been a Moseley institution since the 1860s.

Either side of the passageway are two handsome snugs, one with studded leather seats and oak-panelled walls. And at the front is a proper public bar with scuffed lino and a lengthy line of handpumps.

Purity's Mad Goose, a zesty medium-strength pale ale from rural Warwickshire, seems to be the most popular beer this evening. There are also welcome visitors from further afield, such as Timothy Taylor's Landlord and the aromatic Bishop's Farewell from Oakham Ales.

A huge stag's head of the sort that used to appear on the *Morecambe and Wise Show* is gazing impassively from the doorway as I make my own farewell. 'What do you think of it so far?' 'Could be worse,' its expression seems to say. 'I could be in the Cigar Bar.'

Chris Arnot, 1 August 2015

118 Alcester Road, Moseley, Birmingham B13 8EE (0121 449 4198); theprincemoseley.co.uk

The Old Windmill
Coventry

A voluptuous brunette has just arrived with her partner, asked for a sample of Old Slug porter and evidently found it more acceptable than it sounds. They take a pint apiece to a table opposite the whitewashed former brew house at the Old Windmill.

Unlike other medieval survivors that line Coventry's Spon Street, the Windmill wasn't moved here and reassembled in the post-war years. The core of the building has occupied this spot for six centuries.

You step through the front door on to a passageway of polished, worn stone. To the left is one of three distinctive snugs. There's a welcoming open fire and a shelf lined with books.

Across the passageway is the snuggest of the snugs, occupied this evening by an enormous man with scarcely room for anyone else. Passers-by can at least pause to admire the gleaming brass counter separating this intimate space from the main lounge, where the open fireplace harbours a former priest hole.

At one time there was a piano next to the fire. Sitting adjacent would have been Ma Brown, the matriarch who ran the pub from 1940–67. The Windmill is still known locally as 'Ma Brown's', testimony to the lasting impression that she made in the days when there were courts of terraced housing around the pub.

She encouraged women to pop in. On Sunday lunchtimes housewives would sit in the snugs, podding peas or peeling carrots while sipping 'a dog's nose' – a gin with a half of bitter, though not always in the same glass.

Like all pubs, the Windmill has gone through good times and bad since those days. Currently it's thriving, thanks to licensee Michelle Gilmour.

The Ma Brown *de nos jours* is only 30 but has a real feel for traditional boozers. 'We have a darts team now and I'm trying to set up dominoes and crib teams too,' she tells me as we sit in the third snug with its red and black tiles, chipped here and there by generations of heels, and its black-leaded stove of the sort that once simmered stews for days on end.

I'm savouring the dish of the day, indeed the only dish of every day: a handmade pork pie from the local market washed down by a pint.

Apart from the Old Slug porter, there's Old Speckled Hen and Old Peculier, an old favourite of those with a taste for powerful, dark and complex ales that roll all too seductively over the tongue.

Another Yorkshire gift to beer-lovers, Timothy Taylor's Landlord, is served from a barrel kept in the ground-floor cellar. Not much of a head, which wouldn't go down well East of the Pennines, but the flavour is sublime.

No gin required.

Chris Arnot, 7 November 2015

22–23 Spon Street, Coventry CV1 3BA (024 7625 1717)

The Virgins and Castle
Kenilworth, Warwickshire

E lizabeth I came a-calling at Kenilworth Castle in 1575. She was lavishly entertained by Robert Dudley, the Earl of Leicester, over nineteen days. Despite scurrilous rumours to the contrary, they were just good friends, of course.

Or were they? The 'virgin' queen's sex life remains as shrouded in mystery as Shakespeare's drinking habits. This hasn't stopped The Virgins and Castle giving the impression on its website that young Will from Stratford called in regularly at what was then known as The Two Virgins – for a tankard of ale or a cup of sack, perhaps.

What we know for certain is that Everards Brewery, the pearl of Leicester, has become adept at resurrecting historic inns, and the Virgins and Castle is no exception. Four tiled or flagstoned snugs are warrened away off a 'top bar' framed by weathered beams and offering the full range of Everards ales in tip-top condition. There are also guest beers, a draught cider, a wide range of single malts and a very acceptable lager called Curious Brew made by a Kentish winery using fermented champagne yeast.

Among the top-bar regulars are professors of maths, physics and engineering from the University of Warwick. 'It's amazing what I've learnt while pulling pints,' says manager Martin Trickett.

From the vantage point of the off-duty academics we can see into snug number one with its open fire and shove ha'penny table. Halfpennies are no longer shoved, alas, although the profs play their own version of Spoof, the rules of which are attached to a wall of nicotine yellow. The loser still ends up buying a round.

This is a splendidly higgledy-piggledy pub with well-worn steps between the rooms. Spillages are all too easy. Eyes down for a full pint, particularly if heading for the dining area. Filipino food features prominently, particularly in the evenings. Licensee Laurie Howe came to Kenilworth from Manila, via London, with her late husband.

One of the most popular dishes is the 'crispy pata', which Martin describes as 'like a very big pork scratching'. A pork hock is boiled, roasted and deep fried, served on a wooden slab with pickled veg and garlic rice.

You can crunch crackling to your heart's content – or discontent more likely. 'The pork's pretty good too,' Martin confides, 'once you get to it.' Now he tells me. I've just ordered the 'pork adobo' instead. Still, at least it's a quid cheaper at £11.95, and it feels like the equivalent of Filipino comfort food, soft on the palate while extremely easy on the taste buds.

It goes surprisingly well with a pint of Everards Tiger, a beautifully balanced, robust best bitter, followed by a digestif of the Original Ale. Just a half, thanks. It's hefty enough at 5.2% and, I suspect, infinitely preferable to a cup of sack.

Chris Arnot, 20 December 2014

7 High Street, Kenilworth, Warwickshire CV8 1LY (01926 853737); virginsandcastle.co.uk

The Bear
Stratford-upon-Avon

A chip butty is difficult to eat with decorum. Particularly when there's battered fish in there as well. OK, it's really a 'fish and chip butty', one of several variations on the original that seems to be a *specialité de la maison* on an otherwise more upmarket menu here at the Bear on the banks of the Avon. The fish is white, the chips and batter crisp, the bread lightly toasted to give much-needed firmness to the exterior, particularly as tartar sauce tends to ooze from the sides with every jaw-stretching mouthful.

Very tasty, mind you. Reasonable too, at £3.95. Goes down a treat with a pint of Stratford Gold, a well-balanced session bitter brewed just up the road by the son of one of the regulars. If it's not available, there's usually an alternative Warwickshire ale on sale and Purity's hefty new IPA, Longhorn, is a regular on keg.

Cask-conditioned regulars are Bear Bitter from the North Cotswold Brewery, an amber ale that slips down easily, Wye Valley's deceptively pale yet decidedly full-bodied Butty Bach, and fruity Old Hooky from Hook Norton.

Somebody on the next table is evidently having difficulty deciding what to choose. He's returned from the bar with two halves and three samples, which he swills around the taste-buds like one savouring vintage burgundies.

The late Anthony Burgess, author of an entertaining novel musing on Shakespeare's love life, complained that there were too many places in Stratford that looked like pubs but turned out to be something else. He once wandered into an enticing half-timbered building and was about to order a drink before he realised that he was in a bank.

Well, the Bear doesn't look like a pub from the outside. That's because it's tucked away in the Swan's Nest Hotel.

Inside, however, it's decidedly 'pubby'. A couple are warming themselves in front of a roaring log fire while gazing longingly into each other's smartphones. Those on their way home from work or en route to the RSC across the river are sitting on cushioned settles under wood-panelled walls while swans honk in the gathering darkness.

A group of Grumpy Old Men (their description, not mine) gather here once a month to sup some ale before adjourning to the nearby bistro for discussions on such threats to the blood pressure as the future of *The Sun*'s Page Three girls.

Then there are 'Beck's Boys', who prefer German lager to English ale, despite the abundance of priapic pumps on the bar. Whether Beck's is as well matched with a fish-and-chip butty is a matter of personal taste. As Shakespeare never quite put it, 'Dost thou think, because thou art virtuous, there shall be no more chips and ale?'

Chris Arnot, 21 February 2015

Bridgefoot, Stratford-upon-Avon, Warwickshire CV37 7LT (01789 265540); thebearfreehouse.co.uk

The Victory
Hereford

For most people, a trip to the pub is a bit of an outing. When you visit The Victory, though, you're taking a voyage out to sea.

That's because the whole place is done up like a naval galleon from the time of Admiral Nelson. The bar forms the side of the vessel, with drinks being served from the porthole-dotted lower deck, and a row of cannons protruding from the upper.

Meanwhile, a mass of nets and rigging dangles down over the drinkers, who sit at well-spaced-out tables, on decks that have been vigorously swabbed.

Having gone this far, the pub's management have clearly decided there's no point in stinting on their chosen theme. Hence the profusion of nautically themed signs, reading 'Please Keep Gangway Clear' and 'The Captain's Word Is Law'. Instead of a notice saying 'Ladies' and 'Gents', there is a wall on which appears the word 'Heads' (what real sailors call the conveniences).

And the main bar is just the start of it. Take the long walk from prow to stern (oh, all right, from front to back) of The Victory, and right at the aft end of the establishment is a little stage, where local musicians play not the hornpipe, but something a little louder, judging from the sign which reads: 'Keep Doors Shut When Band Is Playing'.

No question about it, this is very much an alco-pub, rather than a gastropub, the only food on offer being the equivalent of ship's biscuits (nuts, crisps et cetera).

'We have a curry and quiz night on Tuesdays,' explains

the pub's young bo'sun. 'But there's a Thai and two Indian restaurants just up the road, so there's no point us doing meals the rest of the time.'

In short, then, The Victory's assets are liquid, and in that respect, it mints its own money, since it's got its own brewery out the back (now called the Hereford Brewery, formerly the Spinning Dog).

In terms of ales served, we're talking not beer miles, then, but beer feet and inches. There are several different types on offer at any one time, and new crew members are encouraged to find out which is their favourite by ordering the Beer Bat, whereby you can try three different brews for just £2.50.

There's subtle, malty Hereford Dark (4.0% ABV), slightly fruity Best (4.3%), and frothy, appealing Owd Bull (3.9%). And four different types of cider, what with Herefordshire being just as much home to the fermented apple as Somerset.

So, provided you don't overdo it on the drink, you feel when you leave The Victory that you've been on a sea journey, but without the turbulence. Not so much a life on the ocean wave, but at least a lunchtime.

Christopher Middleton, 16 March 2013

88 St Owen Street, Hereford HR1 2QD (01432 274998); open weekends noon–11pm, weekdays 3–11pm

The Bridge Inn
Michaelchurch Escley, Herefordshire

The Bridge is an alliance between the wild west of England and the wilder north-west of Latin America. Landlord Glyn Bufton hails from Herefordshire; his lovely wife, Gisela, from Colombia. They met in London and now live five miles from the foothills of the Black Mountains in the kind of pub that few of us stumble across by chance. The village of Michaelchurch Escley is in the back of beyond.

Worth persevering with satnav or map, mind you, particularly for lovers of good meat. The rump steaks are as thick as the spine of *On the Black Hill*, Bruce Chatwin's 1982 novel, set in similarly bucolic countryside.

With a corona of golden fat around its lower quarters, the meat sprawls across much of the plate, medium rare as requested. There's just enough room for a spiral of crisp onion rings on which a properly grilled tomato perches precariously. Fat but equally crisp chips come in a separate silver 'bucket' along with a little dish of extremely tasty oyster mushrooms.

Pub steaks sometimes constitute a gastronomic assault course. But this one succumbs with comparative ease to knife and molars, bestowing the distinctive flavour of rump without too much jaw-grinding effort. 'Our portions are based on feeding local farmers,' Glyn confides.

Well, they supply the meat and no doubt slake their thirsts with Gwatkin Cider from just down the road. There are two on draught this evening, one of which is called Pyder, a pear-and-apple combo. One of the two remaining handpumps serves our preferred accompaniment. Wye Valley Butty Bach (4.5% ABV) is a hefty premium ale that has travelled all the way from Hereford. From the other pump gushes the same brewery's HPA (4% ABV), a lighter, golden beer ideal for taking on to the terrace as the sun sinks, the weeping willows brushing the surface of Escley Brook.

I'm more than happy in this simply furnished bar with tongue-and-groove panelling, settles around the walls, scrubbed pub tables and a scuffed parquet floor under beams threaded with hops (though cider apples might be more appropriate).

On the door is a poster offering hay for sale. Another advertises a scheme called Flicks in the Sticks, bringing Hollywood to Herefordshire village halls.

In the adjoining bar is an enormous espresso machine serving Colombian coffee. There's also a Colombian pudding on the menu, made with banana bread, toffee, chocolate and nuts topped by a guava bocadillo, which looks like a cough lozenge but tastes much better. Very good with cheese, Gisela assures me. Having seen off a Herefordshire steak and a bucket of chips, I'll just have to take her word for it.

Chris Arnot, 13 July 2013

Michaelchurch Escley, Herefordshire HR2 0JW (01981 510646); thebridgeinnmichaelchurch.co.uk

Wales

The Old Black Lion
Hay-on-Wye, Powys

There is a melancholy about forgotten frontiers, borderlines that history or empire have all but erased. From Trieste in north-eastern Italy, a bus or ferry ride brings you to what used to be the Iron Curtain. The checkpoints are deserted concrete shells; you just stroll through, a little surprised to go unchallenged. Yet the markers of difference remain: casinos, duty-free shops, strip clubs, all tottering towards redundancy as the quaint notion of a boundary between different cultures on opposite sides of the vanished threshold fades away.

Hay-on-Wye, or Y Gelli to give it its Welsh name, is one of the few places in the UK where a national boundary is physical and immediate, something a bit more objective than whizzing past a sign on the motorway. The Dulas Brook, a tributary of the Wye, has carved a steep gully to the east of the town; a hundred yards or so back on the Welsh side, the castle rises brusquely. With a half-decent catapult they could have rained all kinds of flaming righteousness down on the Saesneg, you think. And hard by the castle, snug and old and white, sits the Old Black Lion.

In fact, Hay isn't just a naturally fortified Welsh border town; it's a polis, part of an international confederacy of autonomous statelets, a town of books. Its streets, shops, stalls and – patience – pubs have that peculiar mix of the rustic and the cosmopolitan that you'll find in a hundred pretty country towns, with hedge-funders and sheep-farmers chatting uneasily about sport, politics and local gossip. There are walkers (Offa's Dyke runs close by) and tourists, here for the books, the kayaking, or both. Round the town you'll see what are unmistakably members of the book-dealing tribe: Tattersall check shirts, shiny cords, specs on a cord. A furtive, hurried air, like disgraced clerics. Years of book launches have bred a preference in this sub-species for wine over beer: it's no surprise that the ale offering in the Black Lion is less diverse than in some such places.

As to the pub, it's not so much a pub as a quintessence of pub, a kind of Platonic ideal of pubbishness or pubbitude. It is low and dark, like a cave, with timber posts near-black with age, scrubbed oak tables, wood-burning stoves, a soft pinky-brown effusion of dried hops above the bar.

Even when absent in person, the proprietor Dolan Leighton is represented by her portrait. There is a large, open area, and a small nichey part, and a separate, comfier snug; there is also a small and stark beer garden, from where you can look out across a field to the eastern flank of the valley, and on into another country.

Keith Miller, 16 May 2015

26 Lion Street, Hay-on-Wye, Powys HR3 5AD (01497 820841); oldblacklion.co.uk

The Harp
Old Radnor, Powys

The picnic garden at the front of The Harp does not just have a view: it commands it. Gaze over the top of your mellow Ludlow Gold (4.2% ABV), and you'll see a panorama encompassing huge hills and tiny tumuli, sheep-dotted fields and the rolling Radnor Forest.

It's no wonder that Bronze Age settlers chose to fortify this elevated spot. On a clear day, they would have been able to see for miles around, and get early warning of everything from encroaching enemies to passing mammoths.

It wouldn't be for a few centuries – not until the 15th, to be precise – that work would begin on the lovely stone longhouse that is The Harp today. The building may be less draughty than it was back then, but it still creaks and complains as you walk on its floorboards. And when you're huddled around its log fire, in a high-backed wooden pew, with flagstones under your feet and hops hanging down from the ceiling, you could easily be a Welsh wool merchant, circa 1600, stopping overnight on your way to Hereford market.

Yes, the pub may be painted in tasteful Farrow & Ball green, and dotted with floral displays from a glossy magazine, but it is still attached to its ancient rural roots. Lamb is supplied by a local farmer, beer from the nearby Wye Valley brewery.

And while the place has its fair share of overnight guests from the country's conurbations, who come to sleep in the four-poster bed upstairs, the core clientele is still local.

When they walk in through the door, they don't stride straight up to the bar, as in the city, but pause for a couple of minutes to talk to people already sitting down.

Sometimes they shout in their order from a distance, and amble over only when their pint is poured and it's time to pay. It's not a long journey; there's barely 20 feet between door and bar, and drinks are served from what is not so much a counter as a large hatch.

These size limitations mean there's only room for two ales on tap, which are rotated on a more or less weekly basis (and there are cinema-style trailers for forthcoming attractions).

Food-wise, it's a broad church. As well as serving upmarket scallops with lentil salad (£7) and slow-cooked ham hock (£14) for those who have driven some distance, the pub offers chip butties (£3), jars full of chilli rice crackers (89p), plus six flavours of Tyrells crisps for the short-haul snacker. Not forgetting steak nights every Thursday (£12 for an eight-ounce rump plus free drink).

This part of the UK is short on both railway lines and motorways, so The Harp isn't the easiest place to get to. That said, once you've been, you'll want to come back.

Christopher Middleton, 30 March 2013

Old Radnor, Presteigne, Powys LD8 2RH (01544 350655); HarpInnRadnor.co.uk; closed weekday lunchtimes, open every evening except Mon

The Rose & Crown
Porthcawl, Bridgend

Heaven knows what former landlady Mabel Roberts would make of the Rose & Crown today. Hers was a simple ale house, one of five ranged around the village green at Nottage. Mabel's ale was the best. Or so she claimed, wheezily, as she lugged jugs of the stuff up the steps from the cellar.

She was still alive in 1953. 'We had a picture of her celebrating the Coronation,' says the current manager Hannah Parselle. 'Unfortunately, the frame broke.'

Mabel's Crown Cottage was long ago knocked through into Rose Cottage next door. But some original features remain, including thick interior walls of local stone, a flagstone floor and low, beamed and whitewashed ceilings.

The bar to the left of the front door feels comfortably pubby. More so, I suspect, in the winter months when a log fire roars in the grate at the far end, and locals outnumber visitors staying overnight en route to Swansea or the Gower Peninsula.

This evening there's a *Gavin & Stacey*-ish conversation between the Welsh lilt of three burly men, former prop forwards by the look of them, and the more strident, glottal-stopped tones of a family from Essex. Meanwhile, I'm reacquainting myself with the Reverend James. A dark and brooding character, for sure, with hidden depths and plenty of backbone. Now brewed by Brains of Cardiff, this was once the pride of Buckley's, late of Llanelli. James was a Methodist preacher who took over the company from his father-in-law in the 1820s and somehow managed to

square saving souls with quenching thirsts. Here his beer is
part of a Brains range that includes the ordinary bitter as
well as the more full-bodied SA ('Skull Attack' in student
parlance). All are kept in a condition that surely not even
Mabel would find fault with, even if they're now conveyed
from the cellar to the narrow, intimate bar by handpump
rather than hand.

There's also a guest ale and an ever-changing range of
craft beers from Brains. 'The Big Smoke' is today's offer.
Smoked beer – hmmmm. Think I'll stick to the smoked
trout, and follow up with the rump of lamb: a wise choice,
as it turns out, the lamb having the depth of flavour that
you expect in this neck of the woods. No complaints from
my wife either about her 'Celtic Pride' rib-eye.

By now we're sitting in the restaurant area, close to the
'Cwtch' – Welsh for a snug, since you ask (and a snuggle,
too, as in *Gavin & Stacey*), though this one's for diners
rather than drinkers, or lovers. It's empty this evening,
but the shelves around the edge are crammed with musty
books. *Teach Yourself Ethics*? What Mabel Roberts and the
Reverend James would make of that we can only speculate.

Chris Arnot, 30 August 2014

Heol-y-Capel, Nottage, Porthcawl, Bridgend CF36 3ST (01656
784850); roseandcrownporthcawl.com